GraceWaves
Reflections of Ever-Present Grace

Terry Ellis

GraceWaves: Reflections of Ever-Present Grace
ISBN: Softcover
Copyright © 2017 by Terry Ellis

All rights reserved. No part of this book may be reproduced or transmitted in any form or by any means, electronic or mechanical, including photocopying, recording, or by any information storage and retrieval system, without permission in writing from the publisher.

To order additional copies of this book, contact:

Parson's Porch Books
1-423-475-7308
www.parsonsporch.com

Parson's Porch Books is an imprint of **Parson's Porch & Book Publishers** in Cleveland, Tennessee, which has double focus. We focus on the needs of creative writers who need a professional publisher to get their work to market, **&** we also focus on the needs of others by sharing our profits with those who struggle in poverty to meet their basic needs of food, clothing, shelter and safety.

Dedication

GraceWaves is dedicated to my family: Leslie, Lauren (and Aaron), Greg, Emily Grace, and Beckett. Each one of you helps me see ever-present grace.

Thank you.

Contents

GraceWaves	7
Earlobes for Jesus	11
Good Shame, Bad Shame	14
Harm and Healing from Those Who Are Closest	17
When the Hurt Keeps Hurting	21
Wired for Grace	24
Accidents	27
Singing in the Dead of Night	30
Smiling Back at Heaven	33
Blind Faith? No Such Thing	36
Reasonably Happy	39
God's One Note	43
You're Not the First Person To Do This	46
Comfort and Encouragement	49
Thin Places	52
Scabs or Scars?	58
Change Your Mind, Change Your Life	61
Grace for When You're Not Totally Depraved	65
The Case of the Unwashed Hands	71
Signposts, Not Signs	74
Resentments	77
Choosing to Be Grateful	80
Joy: The Laughter of the Soul	83
So?	86
I'm Not Ok, and That's a Good Place to Start	89

The Glimmer of Hope..92
If We Knew Their Story…..95
John Wayne: Prophet..98
Soul Graffiti.. 101
The Most Important Breakfast Ever...................................... 104

GraceWaves

I first conceived of GraceWaves in a lecture by Dr. Ed Glaze, one of my favorite professors, at New Orleans Seminary in the early 1980's. He loved to teach the Gospel of John, and often said that whenever he read it with expectancy he never failed to find something new. I loved the idea of an inexhaustible Spirit that speaks new truths to us if we have ears to hear and eyes to see.

In his lecture on John 1:16, Dr. Glaze noted the phrase "grace upon grace." John spent three years walking the roads of Galilee and Judea with Jesus. He began with a very basic perception that this man was the Messiah, and grew to realize that He would suffer and die because of His great love for all people and His deep desire to bring us all to God the Father. John saw grace in Jesus, and witnessed it in various forms as Jesus taught, healed, and simply lived with the disciples. Perhaps 50 or more years later as he wrote the gospel bearing his name, John would say of those three years that he and the other disciples received "grace upon grace." Every moment with Jesus offered a new insight into grace. Grace upon grace.

Dr. Glaze suggested the image of the sea where the waves constantly lap over the shore. Never ending, sometimes gentle, and sometimes crashing, the grace of God through Jesus washes over us. I thought then of the idea of GraceWaves. They are constant. You can no more stop gracewaves from God than you can stop the oceans' tides. Grace is an immutably fixed fact of life.

Here's the challenge: much of the time we are too agitated, doubtful, fearful, distracted, etc. to notice the GraceWaves.

Let's change the illustration a bit. As you read this, in the very room where you are, an untold number of electromagnetic waves surround and bombard you. Some of these are very obvious, such as the light from your computer screen or the lamp next to you. Other waves very much less so. However, if you have the right kind of receptor, the right kind of antennae, then you can hear a commercial radio station, pick up a cell phone call, even hear the residual background radiation from the Big Bang. The waves are all around you.

God's intention, I believe, is to transform our spirits to hear His gracewaves. Our search, therefore, and our plea to God, is to tune our hearts and souls to His grace. By our prayers and meditation we align ourselves with the rhythms of God's grace. Then we hear and see gracewaves everywhere. GraceWaves are available to anyone who has expectancy and awareness.

Again, sometimes this is very easy and obvious. In church one morning recently I heard a rendition of a favorite hymn, "Be Thou My Vision." The words never fail to touch my soul and to clarify, for at least a little while, that God is to be my vision. Gracewaves.

My granddaughter, Emily Grace, recently had her fourth birthday party. It was all butterflies, unicorns, princesses, rainbows, cake, and presents. She was so very cute, I thought I would spontaneously combust. She's a wonder of God's creation. Emily Gracewaves.

The stars bear witness to me of the glory of God, and in the dark skies of the Amazon Valley, where I've had the privilege of traveling quite a few times, the Milky Way is so clear. Like the ancient Greeks, I swear I can almost hear the music of the spheres when I behold the heavens. The night sky makes me feel very small until I remember that I am the son and brother of its Creator, then I feel like one of the lords of the universe. Gracewaves.

All of these and more are easy pickings, and because they're ever-present we can always look for them, though it amazes me how often I miss the very obvious glory surrounding me. I doubt I'm alone in this. We all need to refocus on the obvious gracewaves around us.

The harder task, of course, is finding those gracewaves when we're dealing with various forms of the circles of hell that surround us, like Baton Rouge traffic. Here's what I've discovered: my ability to see the glory where only the grit is obvious is directly related to the consistency of my spiritual life. Very simply, the more I pray and mediate, the more I see God's presence. Gracewaves.

Of course, receiving these gracewaves enables me to share the gracewaves. The grace rolls in, and the grace rolls out. This is the rhythm of grace, a glorious calling for each of God's children. Gracewaves.

Approached in this way, life is much less of a struggle, for I'm not trying to bend circumstances to my liking. Life often doesn't cooperate with me. I am then faced with a decision: do I give in to the frustrations of life? Or do I trust in God's power and keep listening for the whispers of the Spirit? When I pause and simply breathe a plea to hear and see God, I've never been disappointed. Gracewaves.

Since 2010 I've written weekly on my website gracewavestoday.com about some facet of grace I've seen in the previous week. This book is a collection of some of my favorites and some of the ones that seem to have been special to my readers. My simple hope and prayer is that, in some small way, they help you to see and hear the grace that God washes over you every moment.

The reader will notice occasional references to my struggle with alcoholism, and an explanatory note may be helpful. I began drinking very late in life, about age 53, quickly became an alcoholic, and spent nearly 3 years in a very dark and dangerous place. I entered treatment and now am in my fourth year of grateful recovery.

I write and speak openly about my experience in churches and organizations all around the country because I want people to know that God's grace finds us in the very darkest places. When we open our hands He gives us His grace, and then weaves that grace into wondrous new chapters in our lives. I began Chrysalis Interventions in a two-fold effort to help people get into recovery and to educate everyone about the disease of addiction and the hope of recovery.

Two final words about these meditations. First, the translations of scriptures are mine when they come from the New Testament, for I still retain a fairly decent proficiency in Greek from my doctoral studies. Alas, my Hebrew is far too rusty, and all Old Testament scriptures are from the RSV.

Second, the reader will notice that all pronouns referring to God are capitalized. The ancient scribes had the habit of abbreviating references to God by writing only the first and last letters of the name, both letters capitalized, and a line over the top. They called it *nomina sacra*, or sacred name. It was a means of revering God in the text. I've always liked that idea, and capitalized pronouns are my form of *nomina sacra*.

Grace,

Dr. Terry Ellis
February 20, 2017

Earlobes for Jesus

"Only let your manner of life be worthy of the gospel of Christ."
Philippians 1:27

She knew precisely how to begin the conversation. "Daddy, I have something to tell you. I hope you're not mad, but I want you to know." The call was from my 15-year-old daughter who was returning home from a week at a youth camp during which she was challenged to live mightily for God, embrace what is good, and eat the cafeteria food. She was on the bus about to leave for the day-long trip home when she made THE CALL.

"I have something to tell you." At this point I, like any parent, am riffling through all the possibilities of what the "something" may be. 99.999% of them are bad. Grateful that I got the call instead of her mother, I calmly said, "All right. What is it?"

"I got my ears pierced." Now, at this point when you have begun with "I've got something to tell you that might upset you" and you end with an ear piercing, you oddly feel a measure of relief. I still had enough wits about me to ask, "What do you mean? Your ears are already pierced."

Ear-piercing is one of those parental tests you go through with a daughter, hopefully only with your daughter. Fathers generally feel that age 30 is a good time for a daughter to do anything that might make her remotely attractive to the opposite sex. I had been through this challenge. Her ears were pierced. The sun rose the next day, and no mob of hyper-hormonal boys were beating on the front door. I passed that test. So ear-piercing on a youth trip? You can understand my confusion.

"Double piercing," she explained. All right. I get the picture. Two holes. "Where's the second one?" I asked, genuinely uncertain. She answered with that tone that made me feel like a Neanderthal, as if I should know the nuances of double-piercing etiquette. "Right next to the first one." I didn't know. Accepted double-piercing form precludes the second piercing anywhere but the lobe. How very droll of me not to know better.

She went on to explain that at a wee morning hour she and a handful of her cohorts became impressed that they needed to be more dedicated Christian girls, and that as a sign of their devotion they would pierce their ears, excuse me, double pierce, their ears. The second stud or ring or whatever you call the subsequent ornament would serve as a visible reminder to them of their collective commitment. She told me they even had a worship service afterward, read scripture, sang worship hymns. I am not making any of this up.

All right. Deep breath. At this point, amazement was equaled by amusement. Optimist that I am, my thoughts in rapid succession were something like: "it was only her ear lobe, not some other body part," "no chains are involved," "it won't look like bread mold heading south by the time she's thirty," "how the devil did you do this?", "do the words 'sterile conditions' mean anything to you?", and "it's not any of the other thousand things that could have been much worse."

Also, the practice is somewhat Biblical. Stay with me, I had to bring Leslie along slowly on this point. Some type of physical sign as a symbol of devotion is not unusual in the Bible. Paul shaved his head as a vow to God during one of his missionary journeys (Acts 18). Four brethren did the same in Jerusalem (Acts 21). The Nazirite vow, of which the previous two are examples, is described in Numbers 6, but can also involve letting one's hair grow. And who can forget Abraham and his "sign of the covenant?" I'm pretty sure Abraham had been through something like a sleep-deprived youth camp prior to that minor surgery.

To Lauren's credit she told me that she "racked her brain" trying to remember if I had ever explicitly told her that she couldn't get a double piercing. I have to admit, I had never explicitly said "do not ever skewer any body part after midnight on a church trip." The law was on her side. And trust me, I began compiling that list immediately.

Another deep breath. She was not the first girl to do something like this. Some of my present readership can hearken back to days of pins and corks and conditions less antiseptic than present day boutiques. So it could have been worse. And really, much of the intent was quite good, even if the expression was a bit questionable.

So, I was glad she and her friends, newly pierced and all, had a good time at camp. I was not angry or disappointed. In fact, I loved their passion. I recalled days when, in a new-found fervor, I was willing to do anything for God, and I pray for that zeal today. We all need conviction combined with courage. And some type of sign is good, though let me suggest a new Bible or perhaps a bracelet.

Our prayer should always include the commitment to meet God's ever-fresh offer of grace with a gentle zeal to honor Him in all we do. Yes, that will be my prayer.

And that her lobes won't fall off.

Good Shame, Bad Shame

"Neither do I condemn you." John 8:11

Shame. That must have been the main feeling of the woman caught in adultery when she was dragged before Jesus. She had been caught in the very act by men who probably set her up as a test for this new rabbi with His notions of grace and easy ways with sinners. "Let's see how He handles a real sinner!"

The woman was guilty. Of course, equally so was the man, the ostensibly married man. It does take two to tango, or to commit adultery. We never hear anything about him. But let's be clear, if we focus solely on the woman and her conduct, she broke a commandment. This is not trivial. Sins hurt people. Mainly they hurt the sinner.

So shame can serve a good purpose when it alerts us that we are out of alignment with God and His purpose for us. But let's be careful even with this well-conceived idea.

One of the great misconceptions about sin is that it simply offends God that we broke one of His rules, that we make Him angry. This upward concept of sin, that we must avoid making God angry, is so far from the truth. What God wants us to avoid is hurting ourselves and other people. He loves us deeply, and He doesn't want anything bad to happen to us. Sin hurts, and when all spiritual systems are working correctly, shame creates humility and brings us back to God's grace. That's good shame.

The focus of the story in John 8, however, isn't on good shame. The focus isn't really on the notion of "go and sin no more." That's not a bad point, of course, but I don't think it's the main point.

The real focus is on how God handles our shame.

Think of the scene after all the men dropped their rocks and dispersed. The woman stood alone before Jesus. Now we know more than she did, and what we know is very important. Jesus would later say "If you have seen Me, you have seen the Father" (John 14:9). So the woman was standing, drenched in shame, real, accurate, appropriate shame, before God.

What happened next? We all know the story. Jesus, removed her shame. "Neither do I condemn you." God did not condemn her.

If we're dealing with real shame, then we need to hear the heart of the gospel. God is not the giver of shame. He is the remover of shame. "Though your sins be as scarlet, they shall be white as snow." We can be free from shame and live the life God created for us. He delights in doing this for us!

But what about bad shame? This is the shame that comes from other people, that has nothing to do with your actions, but ends up shaping your identity. Bad shame is the chronic condemnation by people who should have loved and affirmed you. Bad shame is the actions of others that somehow make you feel dirty, or worthless, or humiliated. Bad shame is the rejection by those who should be embracing you.

Bad shame is a whispered guilt. The first two letters sound like a secret. "Shhh! Don't tell. Don't repeat."

Bad shame is also a shouted verdict. "FOR SHAME! Don't ever forget what you have done!"

I believe bad shame is far more prevalent than good shame. It's a drenching condemnation we carry around with us. It goes to the very heart of our identities, isolates us, and holds us back in a thousand different ways. It's a quintessential soul-sickness.

And that brings me back to the woman. What happened after the story ended? It's not hard to imagine. The woman was free. Free from fear, guilt, and shame–and all of this directly from God.

Wonderful!

Now what about all the people in her community? Do you think they really had a spiritual insight to their own shame? Do you think they embraced and shared grace? I seriously doubt it.

The woman turned from a gracious God to a still condemning community. I doubt anything changed in that village. They still thought of her as an adulteress. I imagine she was marginalized for the remainder of her life by most people who knew her story.

Shame is an easy currency. People throw it around and spend it at others' expense all the time. You likely have been the target. But just because someone throws shame at you doesn't mean you have to stand still and let it hit you.

That sums up the decision the woman had to make. She still lived in the village where people had falsely accused her. Would she listen to the critics who reminded her of her failures? Or would she listen to the God who reminded her of her future? What voices would she listen to?

What voices do you listen to?

It's an enormously difficult task, an act of sustained will, to block out the voices that shout bad shame. The good news is the Bible powerfully depicts a God who bears away shame. You may be feeling shame from past chapters of your life, but God always offers forgiveness, and by asking for it we feel its full effect. The bad shame you carry? Let God take that away too. It comes from broken people who inflict you with pain from their wounds. It's not yours. Never was.

I was recently reminded of some sound theology from Rascal Flatts that applies to shame, good and bad. "I've been burdened with blame (shame), trapped in the past for too long. I'm movin' on." That's the gospel in action. That's the full effect of grace

Harm and Healing from Those Who Are Closest

"So Joseph said to his brothers, 'Come near to me, I pray you.' . . . And he kissed his brothers and wept upon them, and after that his brothers talked with him." Genesis 45:4, 15

These words come from one of the most moving scenes in all of scripture. But first, let's review the events that led up to it.

In a move that might be understood and even endorsed by many elder siblings, Joseph's brothers sold him into slavery when he was a boastful teen. He endured terrifying years of threats, disappointments, and even imprisonment. He kept his faith, however, and eventually ascended to the right hand of Pharaoh.

All those long years his brothers thought him gone forever and probably dead. They told their father that he had been killed by a lion and dragged off. Then during a famine in Canaan, the brothers journeyed to Egypt for grain. Joseph, having found out about their journey, concealed his identity and demanded they meet with him.

The scene is perfect for revenge and retribution. The brothers, no doubt baffled and fearful at having to meet with such a high official, acceded to all his demands. Eventually, in one of the most moving scenes in the Bible, Joseph revealed his identity, forgave, and paved the way for reconciliation with his brothers. The relationships came full circle and became stronger and healthier. Joseph, who had likely been an arrogant youth, became forgiving and understanding. The brothers, driven in earlier years by jealousy, had tender hearts that were open to grace.

Ironically, but indisputably, much of the pain we experience in life comes from the people closest to us. Family and friends are on the inner circle, and thus have many opportunities to reach out and strike. You can forget about a rude stranger, but you will bear the scars of a harsh family member for a lifetime. Your heart will ache when you recall a friend that is no longer a friend. Close relationships offer great blessings, but also the potential for great pain. Vulnerability is a function of proximity.

This vulnerability is the basic risk of love. Both grief and hurt only occur when we take the risk of opening up and letting someone come close. We often pay a steep price for deep relationships. The harm comes from those closest to us.

Genevieve Adams, a dear friend, wrote "it's good to remember that people often hurt one another out of their own dysfunction and pain." That's hard to remember when the bruises are fresh and the wounds still bleed, but pain is like an electrical current that can flow through generations. Psychologists have long been warning that trauma of all kinds wreaks tremendous havoc. We're now becoming aware that trauma can begin very early in life. A mother's high stress levels affect a developing fetus. A chaotic environment crucially impacts neural development in the infant and young child. So great is this affect that we can say that many chronically hurting people never had a chance for a peaceful and reasonably happy life, and so they eventually end up hurting others.

More ironically, however, healing often comes through those same relationships. I walk very carefully through this minefield and ask that you pay close attention. Some people have suffered tremendous damage at the hands of a parent or sibling, and as much as they might want it to be so, some relationships will never become healthy. Many times, we must close the books on a relationship, literally asking God to move out of our lives, and our minds, unhealthy influences. The false yearning to repair every relationship is every bit as toxic as the active harm we originally suffer. Setting boundaries and barriers is not a lack of grace, but a commitment to wisdom.

Much of the time, however, God will work on your heart and the heart of the estranged family member or friend, and provide an opportunity for reconciliation. God did that for Joseph and his brothers, and Joseph likely would never have been whole without the story in Genesis 45. The same relationship that caused the damage is often the same relationship that provides the restoration.

Firmly now in the autumn of my life, I've often witnessed harm and healing from the very same people. Many times forlorn parents and grandparents will pronounce a final, sad verdict on a prodigal child. Or the jagged, raw pain of betrayal and anger may even lead a person to swear by God-almighty that they never want to see that person again! The estrangement often comes during late teens and twenties when the son or daughter feels the flush of freedom and a false but heady self-confidence that produces disdain for other family members.

In most cases I know of, however, both parties eventually come to a new understanding, acceptance, and love of one another. This new love is stronger and healthier than previously. This takes time and, because of that, patience. But there is hope! Like the tender root of a tree that over the years breaks through concrete and rock, grace finds a way to crack through the hardest heart.

The most common mistake I make and see with regard to toxic relationships is the drive to change the other person by proving them wrong, or pathologically loving them to the point of trying to force reconciliation. This timing is best left to God, and our focus needs to be on the person in the mirror. An interesting variation of the Serenity Prayer reads, "God grant me the serenity to accept the person I cannot change, courage to change the person I can, and the wisdom to know that I'm that person."

Because of the potential for reconciliation, we should cultivate a gentle and forgiving spirit. Joseph probably was not always open to this possibility, but God worked with him. Whether you ever get a chance for reconciliation, you still do not want to carry with you a burden of bitter disappointment and anger. Forgive, pray a blessing, and move forward, always open to the opportunity God may provide. As Paul wrote, "If possible, so far as it depends on you, live peaceably with all," (Rom. 12:18).

You can close some doors on unhealthy relationships, but you don't necessarily need to double bolt them. In the same vein, don't feel the need to keep pounding on doors that have been closed to you. God will provide for your healing, and your healing is not dependent on anyone else's decisions. Grace truly is sufficient. If the person who hurt you chooses to be part of that grace solution, then the blessing will be for him or her also. You may occasionally knock, perhaps through a card or brief phone call, but do not make your peace contingent upon a person who historically demonstrates unreliability.

Grace is so infinitely pervasive, so wonderful ubiquitous that you never know where it might come from or from whom. Do not set your hopes on the estranged family member turning around and embracing you and asking for forgiveness. But do not be surprised if some day, many years in the future, that does occur. Just do not mandate that as the only way God can give you grace for your healing.

When the Hurt Keeps Hurting

"Bless those who curse you, pray for those who abuse you."
Luke 6:28

Previously I wrote about the very real possibility that the people who have hurt you may be the ones through whom God brings healing. As Joseph was reconciled to his brothers, I have seen fractured relationships restored. Husband/wife, parent/child, friend/friend, etc. God has a remarkable way of bringing people around, working His grace into their lives, "softening" them, so that they come to a point where they ask for forgiveness or offer it where previously it was withheld.

Whenever I have written about this topic I receive multiple responses from people who are burdened in their lives with close relations who have hurt them and show no sign whatsoever of any interest in apology, a request for forgiveness, and certainly not reconciliation. Let me stress that these questions arise from conscientious Christians who (1) would do anything to facilitate reconciliation or (2) are uncertain of their ongoing responsibility in the face of continual spite or indifference from the person who originally hurt them.

Simply put, what do we do when the hurt keeps hurting? And especially when the source is from someone who should have been a blessing?

First, forgive, pronounce a blessing, and move on. This threefold piece of advice reflects most of what I find in the New Testament concerning this challenge. The verse for this GraceWaves is from Jesus Himself, and isrepeated in many forms throughout the New Testament. Thus we know that forgiveness is a non-negotiable Christian responsibility. If you are trying to retain hard feelings, and construct a case for withholding forgiveness, then frankly you have doomed yourself to a wrestling match with God you eventually will lose.

Forgiveness is not sometimes hard, it's <u>always</u> hard. Forgiveness is costly, particularly when the object of your forgiveness demonstrates no inclination to wanting it. I would not for a moment suggest that all forgiveness is of the same level of challenge. Some hurts are very deep, even unspeakably evil. Coming to a point of offering forgiveness for some acts takes a very long time, and if you are struggling to forgive you must not compound the problem with unnecessary guilt and self-recrimination. Make it a matter of prayer, and trust that God in His time, and in cooperation with your spirit, will enable you to offer genuine forgiveness.

Pronouncing a blessing, even on those who curse you, is another familiar New Testament teaching. Jesus knew this step also would be hard, and that is why He reminds us in the Sermon on the Mount that God makes the sun to rise on the evil and the good, and the rain to fall on the just and unjust (Matt. 5:45). We bless, not as a function of the other person's goodness, but simply because we all need blessing and none of us have earned it. To pronounce a blessing on difficult and even hostile people in some way acknowledges that you do not know what has made that person so difficult or hostile. You are not waiting for them to change or setting preconditions. You simply bless because this act is very God-like.

Now, moving on is where some fine Christians struggle mightily. They may wonder if moving on amounts to giving up on a person, which, of course, Jesus never did. But let's look at Jesus a little more closely. He did not chase after the Pharisees trying to "patch things up." Neither in the parable did the father chase after the prodigal son trying to talk him into returning. Yes, Jesus died on a cross for all these hard and evil people, but God did not give you either the ability or responsibility to give your life for someone who is uninterested in the grace you offer. If you struggle here you may need to face the reality that you are expecting a blessing from someone who is simply unable or unwilling to give it, and that is not your fault. You may also need to prayerfully consider why you maintain such a fundamentally unhealthy (for you!) expectation. Move on.

Second, remember "you have been crucified with Christ and it is no longer you who live, but Christ who lives in you" (Gal. 2:20). Frankly, Paul's words here are beyond me, but they bring us to a realm so profoundly mysterious and infinitely important that we must make some effort to understand them.

The union of you with Christ is a thrilling teaching in the New Testament and has a special application in forgiving those who have intensely hurt you. Christ knows better than anyone what it is like to love those who do not return love. He knows the depth of rejection in ways you never can. Now I am not suggesting "you haven't had it nearly so bad as Jesus, so get over it." Not at all. I am simply pointing out the fact that your union with Christ enables and compels you to "share in His sufferings" (Rom. 8:17, Phil. 3:10).

God has a way, through the presence of Christ in you, of helping you endure a continual hurt. You certainly cannot change other people to make them more receptive to your offer of grace, but you can pray for God to continue His work in you to make you more receptive to His offer of grace. I believe this spiritual discipline is a key to your moving on. When you have trouble with hurtful people, remember the cross. I am sure that is at least part of what Paul meant.

People who should have blessed you often hurt you. In fact, the closer someone is to you, the deeper the cuts. But the story of grace is still being written in every life. Let the Author do His work. Continually hand to Him your thorniest problems, especially when the hurt keeps hurting.

Wired for Grace

"There is no fear in love, but perfect love casts out fear."
1 John 4:18

I may be biting off more than I can chew with this topic, or more than will be remotely interesting to many of you, but this is my book, so I can do what I want.

Let me start with a conversation I had a while back with a young woman named Amy. She had been raised in a similar religious environment to mine, but now had a very uncertain relationship with her parents. Grace was not the theme in her family. Judgmental attitudes and a very conditional love dominated.

After she spoke for a while I simply said, "none of that comes from a good and loving God." This seemed to be a great relief to her.

I've had countless conversations like this over the years, and frankly I'm always left a little puzzled. How do people miss the theme of deep grace in the Bible, especially in the life and teachings of Jesus? God is love, according to John, who added that perfect love casts out all fear. So why is there so much fear and so little trust? Why is there so much tendency to control and so little willingness to accept? In short, why is there so much legalism and so little grace?

In part, the answer lies in the very structures of the brain, that marvelous intersection of heaven and earth. At its best, this wondrous collection of interrelated structures and regions literally helps us "see" a God of peace and grace. At its worst, it sentences us to a life that cringes from a god of thunder and lightning, and is likely to lead us to sling a few bolts of condemnation ourselves.

Very simply, the brain is actually three brains. To illustrate, hold up your fist. From top of the wrist down is the brain stem. It is responsible chiefly for the autonomic functions of the body such as breathing, heart rate, blood pressure, and some fine motor coordination. It is sometimes called "the reptilian brain" because it is the most primal structure of the brain, and focuses on fundamental matters of survival.

The fist (with the fingers wrapped around the thumb) is the midbrain and of chief concern here is the limbic system (the thumb). Here we have the capacity to form and store memories and to feel some very raw emotions including fear, anxiety, anger, etc. The sex drive is here, as is the autonomic response to fight, flight, or freeze when threatened. The amygdala, a small structure in the limbic system, is particularly central to the formation and expression of anger and fear. When you see an angry person, even the one in the mirror, you're seeing someone whose amygdala is fired up and taking over. Much of what takes place here is unconscious and reflexive.

The third part of the brain is represented by your other hand, which you take and cover your fist. This is the forebrain or neo-cortex, the familiar looking part of your brain with all the folds. This is the most recent evolutionary development (thus neo). Especially in the frontal lobe of the neo-cortex, we find wisdom and love and most clearly perceive and interact with God.

Without the neo-cortex we are little more than bratty, self-centered, angry adolescents. When the brain is fully engaged the neo-cortex has an executive function that keeps us from embracing out-of-control emotions and out-of-control drive for sex or food. The neo-cortex makes us human in the highest sense.

What I suggest is that many times we struggle to move beyond a god of fear and anger because these emotions are so deeply rooted in our brains. They are almost default responses. It's far easier, for example, to condemn your enemy than to love and pray for your enemy. The former is driven by the lower brain's fear and desire to protect. The latter requires conscious reasoning and commitment.

Legalism is grounded in the limbic system. Grace comes from the neo-cortex. Theologically, we are in a constant struggle to embrace grace over legalism, because neurologically we are in a constant struggle of the neo-cortex over the limbic system.

Amy suffered from a theological limbic-hangover that came from the people who gave her her first image of God; that is, her parents. Like all of us, she needed to listen to the higher call of a whispered grace that is ultimately reasonable and freeing. But it takes effort and will.

I'm not saying only smart people embrace grace. Grace, thankfully, has nothing to do with intellect. I'm saying that perfect love is grace, and perfect love casts out fear. We have to think our way beyond anger and fear, and God has given us all the capacity to do so. Living with an angry god stirs up angry emotions. This is bad neural hygiene, or stinkin' thinkin'.

To live in grace, to live freely, we simply must focus our prayer lives on a God who wants to cast out all fear from our lives. Try this: Close your eyes, take a few minutes to center down or become quiet, and then quietly repeat for a few minutes "perfect love casts out fear." This simple meditation literally quiets the angry and fearful parts of your brain, and begins to engage the regions where God speaks most clearly. Frankly, it's indisputable—the perfect alchemy of physiology and theology. Try it.

And remember that Jesus never once acted like an angry fundamentalist. He was gentle and gracious with sinners who came to Him with their brokenness. In fact, He consistently reserved His harshest rebukes for the most religious and narrow-minded people of His day.

Fear is corrosive, on others but mainly on ourselves. Think your way to a God of grace. It's the way He made you.

Accidents

"They who wait upon the Lord shall renew their strength, they shall mount up with the wings of eagles." Isaiah 40:21

Remember the exhilaration of driving alone for the first time? In Kentucky, where I was raised, you had to be 16 before you got your permit and then had to wait at least 30 days before the driver's test. As I recall, I went the day of my birthday for my permit and the 31st day for my exam, a youthful zeal my mother did not share.

My first stop was Mom's work place. She was suitably proud and told all of her coworkers who looked at my goofy picture and vowed to be watchful for me on the roads, etc. Anxious to be off on my own, I told her where I was going and when I'd be home. Free at last, I ventured into the tangled late afternoon traffic in a Ford Galaxy 500 that was about the size of a minor aircraft carrier.

I returned home at the appointed time to find my mother dabbing tears, as she often did over us children for no reason other than we were in a world that was simply waiting to pounce on the Ellis clan. Mom wouldn't go into Mammoth Cave for fear that it was just waiting untold millennia for the opportunity to fall on an Ellis. I'm not making this up.

The cause of her tears this time was a minor fender bender on the road outside her place of work after I left…about an hour after I left. Mind you I was nowhere in the vicinity of the accident and had returned home unscathed. Nevertheless, that set Mom to ponder the certainty that the Fates were planning my fiery demise on the highways at any moment.

Mom was a classic worrier, but I don't mock her or deride her for that. I used to laugh at her parental anxiety, but then I had kids who turned 16 and began driving. I believe it was after Gregory got his license that I took him immediately to the insurance agent for "the talk" that was much more important than where babies come from.

I wanted him to know how much his new freedom was costing me and how grateful and careful he should be. Yes, I really did that.

John, the agent at the time, waited until Gregory left the room. He turned to me and said, "You know he's going to have an accident, don't you?" He quoted the statistics and told me to be prepared to find out that it would not be the end of the world, and to pray that no one would get hurt–which they usually do not. Good advice.

Of course Grego did have an accident, a minor one. So did Lauren. Both knocked off so many side-view mirrors that I could have paid off my mortgage by now. And both apparently learned from the minor accidents and are today safe and proficient drivers. I'm sure they, like me, became better drivers because of the early mistakes they made.

When it comes to life, I have this perspective retroactively. God has it proactively. He knows the mistakes we make are not the final verdict on the value of our lives. In fact, God knows that my mistakes in life bring me one more step toward His vision for me, and that's quite remarkable.

As reluctant as we are to endure failure and pain, surely one of the central lessons of the gospel is that the good news involves dealing rightly with the bad news. When it comes to sin and suffering, the persistent and irritating refrain of the Word is that hardships are the pathway to peace. You don't get there without collecting a few scars along the way. It's just not possible.

But God's economy of grace changes the whole equation. Though I might see my mistake or misfortune, whether by my own hand or simply as the result of living in a jagged and broken world, as one more piece of condemnation, God sees it as one more step to my completion. God regards my falls as opportunities for growth, not confirmation that He's wasted time on me. I bemoan the fact that I've fallen in the same way for the sixteenth time, for example, but

God rejoices because He knows I will learn to live the right way after my seventeenth time of failing in the same way.

This is raw, unfiltered, straight from the Source grace. That's why it sounds too good to be true. Until a soul vibrates perfectly with the eternal rhythms of grace, then grace will always sound a little suspicious. Most of us fear that if everything is so freely forgiven, then what's to keep us from piling up the numbers and airily saying that's just one more step to my completion?

The answer is twofold. First, there's nothing free about forgiveness. The cross was costly. Just because we didn't have to pay the price doesn't mean that grace is free.

Second, and this is the consistently overlooked facet of "graceology," grace has a certain gravity. It draws us, and the closer we get to the Source, the more speed we pick up. Receiving grace doesn't mean we'll cast off every moral restraint and live like heathens. Grace is the soil of both humility and gratitude, not licentiousness.

I'm not consistently soaring yet, as Isaiah promised. Too many accidents. But the accidents don't mean I'll never get my wings. And I think I'm learning, as God knows well, that unbroken success just inflates my ego. The accidents, the falls, the failures, those are God's real opportunities.

So I have to accept that most days I just limp along, but that's all right. Grace will help me one day to limp into a circle of light, and then I will soar. But not yet. Until then, it's one day at a time, one mistake at a time, one victory at a time, and grace for every moment. Perhaps in God's sight, all my mistakes are not really accidents at all.

Singing in the Dead of Night

"Where is God my Maker, who gives songs in the night?"
Job 35:10

[The following is for my 16-year-old granddaughter, who's only 4 right now.]

> Blackbird singing in the dead of night,
> Take these broken wings and learn to fly,
> All your life, You were only waiting for this moment to arrive.
>
> Blackbird singing in the dead of night,
> Take these sunken eyes and learn to see.
> All your life, You were only waiting for this moment to be free.
>
> Blackbird fly, Blackbird fly,
> Into the light of a dark black night.
>
> The Beatles

Dear Emily Grace,

When you were little, you knew and loved all the typical childhood songs: Baa Baa Black Sheep, Muffin Man, Twinkle, Twinkle Little Star, etc. You sang them all with the delightful enthusiasm of new discovery. Repeatedly. You excelled at the encore. Repeatedly.

Wanting to add to your repertoire, one day I sang for you the old Beatles' song Blackbird, and you loved it. Maybe it was the choreography I ad libbed. We flapped like blackbirds and opened our eyes wide to see. This became one of your favorites, and we played it, no surprise here, repeatedly. I cherish the memory of turning my rearview mirror down just a bit so we could watch each other sing and flap and see while I drove.

Now that you've firmly entered the turbid waters of female adolescence I want you to know why I sang that song for you and why I'm so glad it became one of your favorites. You need right now what this song is about, and though I've doubtless talked to you about it over the years I want you to have in writing what I want you to glean from it.

First, let's establish the importance of meaning and interpretation. Some texts, lyrics, stories, poems, songs, and paintings are imbued with deep meaning. They call to you, and invite you to a deeper, or higher, life. You'll have to seek this out, for you live in a world that too often shouts its superficiality. God, who wonderfully made you, created in you a need for significance that shouting will never fulfill. Finding places and times to be still and listen and watch is vital. The very good news is that you'll always find what you're truly looking and listening for. Always. Good or bad. Deep or shallow. I hope you always make time to look for the divine shimmering around you and listen for the song of eternity. Seek these.

Now back to the song. Singing birds are wondrous, but how often do you hear a blackbird singing in the dead of night? Never. I suppose there might be some obscure specie that sings at midnight, but certainly not the typical blackbird. They sing to the sunrise and throughout the day.

But the blackbird in the song is singing in the dead of night. Why? Because it needed to, of course. It sings like it's the dawn even though its surrounded by darkness. It does what it was created to do in spite of the darkness, and in defiance of the darkness.

The same idea applies to the broken wings. Frankly, I've never known a bird to fly with broken wings. In nature, I'm afraid that's the end of the bird. But our brave bird learns to fly even when it appears impossible. And he learns to see even with sunken (unseeing) eyes.

Sometimes, Emily Grace, your wings will get broken. You won't achieve the heights you dreamed of, and you might not feel like there's any use in trying. You'll be tempted to sit in your nest, in the dark, and "beweep your outcast state." Many people do.

What I want for you, dear Emily Grace, is to be the blackbird. Don't let broken wings, sightless eyes, or a dark black night keep you from being the daughter your heavenly Father created you to be. Yes, the dark black nights are real and sometimes terrifying, but they don't define you or determine your destiny. God has already done that. He has given you the ability to see His light even in the frightening gloom. With faith and trust in this smiling God you'll be able to sing, and fly, and see.

This is not easy. Even our blackbird struggled for quite a while, for he had waited for this moment to arrive and to be free. You likely will have many occasions where the evidence for goodness, love, and grace looks pretty thin, or even damning. Doubt will keep you nest-bound. But there will come a moment of clarity when you will decide to be done with lesser things and summon the courage to try to fly even when everyone around you is shouting for you to give it up. God loves this kind of courage! Only by taking the risk, again and again, will you learn that you never lost your ability to fly.

One final thing. God has a delightful habit of peeking out at us from unlikely places. He winks and smiles as if to say "I'm always here, and this is just a little reminder." The reminder might be that story, poem, or painting I mentioned earlier. Or it might be a sunrise, or the stars, or a flower. It could be this little essay written by your grandfather many years ago. Maybe this is what you needed to get you out of the nest and flying and singing again. Fact is, God surrounds us with reminders. Be one who sees and hears.

Long ago I saw the joy in your eyes. It is a gift from God, and you will learn to cherish it and share it (which is the only way it grows). Trust me, people need your joy. Remember it, and fly.

I'll love you forever,

Gandy

Smiling Back at Heaven

"Are not two sparrows sold for a penny? And not one of them will fall to the ground without your Father knowing it." Matthew 10:29

This familiar verse has spawned a very familiar hymn. "His Eye Is on the Sparrow" is a soul-full of comfort based on this text. Jesus taught that because God cares for sparrows, then certainly He will care for you. The way we've traditionally understood this is that a sparrow does not die (fall to the ground) without God's knowledge.

That's good to know. I suppose anytime I come across a dead bird I should think about this text. Maybe I should start thinking about it when I see live birds. Let me explain.

Years ago something started bothering me about this text. Random thoughts about it rattled around for a while until the familiar became a little disturbing. The nub of the problem for me was that while it is somewhat comforting to know that God observes the death of a sparrow, it's a little curious to think that He only takes notice when they fall to the ground. What about their lives?

Let's look closely at the words Jesus used. The New Testament was written in Greek. While Jesus probably spoke and understood Greek, as well as Hebrew and probably Latin, the language of everyday life in the first century was Aramaic. Jesus almost certainly spoke Aramaic when He taught and conversed. He spoke Aramaic when He said the words of the verse above.

The Greek word for "fall" literally means to fall, and can imply a death, as in fall to the ground. The underlying Aramaic word, however, might be better translated here as "to light," as in "to light upon the ground." The meaning then would be that God notices not just the death of a sparrow, but its everyday life. He watches as it lights upon the ground to eat or gather twigs for its nest and as it raises its young. He sees it sing in the sunlight, and fluff up every bit of its feathery insulation trying to stay warm in the cold.

I love that image of God! The Creator, I don't think, simply put together a bunch of atoms into the shapes of man and beast and plant and then cast them upon the earth. The Living One is The Life, and "that which was created in Him was life." So God, I think, in a mysterious way is both the source and the continual inhabitant of all life.

Think about that. "To all life Thou givest, to both great and small; in all life Thou livest, the true life of all" is how that great hymn "Immortal, Invisible, God Only Wise" has it. All of life, in its infinite variety is unsurprisingly a reflection and direct expression of God, the source of all life. So God knows about every sparrow from egg to grave.

Of course, the real point of the text is that *we* are important to God, vastly important to God. God takes an interest in our going out and our coming in. He forms us in the womb and walks with us through the darkest valley or meets us in the clouds. We are bearers of His image, a little bit of the Creator in every one of us.

Jesus emphatically and repeatedly tried to impress on us that God's interested in all aspects of our lives. This interest is not an overbearing vigilance. He's neither "the resident policeman" nor the frowning judge. Rather His interest is a gracious offer to be involved in our lives, throughout the day, every day. In His infinite wisdom, joy, and love, God can watch a sparrow go about its daily task and take delight in that little puff of a blessing. Even more importantly, and this is Jesus' point, God watches us and gently guides, blesses, and takes delight in each one of us.

Perhaps the chief idol people fearfully worship is the grim one that loves us in a contractually obligated sort of way but certainly isn't happy about it. That's so far from the truth that it would be laughable if not for the fact that it keeps so many people in chronic fear. If we think seriously for ten minutes about the fact that God came in Jesus, and the way He conducted Himself when He was here, then we are bound to realize that God seems to like us. I think Jesus smiled a lot, because the Father smiles a lot.

The filaments of God's grace work deeply into every moment of the day, so that no single moment is ever bereft of the touch of divinity. God lovingly watches and cares for us. We are not overlooked, forgotten, or neglected, even though many events and currents in life can make us feel that way. Our lives are important to God. "Your smiles, your frowns, your ups, your downs" are all familiar to Him. We have a joyous, loving, heavenly Father who enjoys us, loves to be a part of our lives, and can bless each moment.

We truly can take one day at a time and enjoy one moment at a time when we remember that is all God has promised. Let's not leave Him out of this moment or the next. God longs to be involved and bring that unique, heavenly joy into every moment. He is a smiling God. Our best response is to look toward heaven and smile back.

Blind Faith? No Such Thing

"By faith Abraham obeyed when he was called to go out to a place which he was to receive as an inheritance; and he went out, not knowing where he was to go." Hebrews 11:8

I ran across a familiar phrase this past week: blind faith, as in "some things you just have to accept on blind faith." I don't buy it. I really don't believe in blind faith. We never have to accept a situation or direction on blind faith.

The closest example we have in the Bible of someone having to act on blind faith is probably Abraham. When God called him to leave Haran, God did not tell him where he was going. We can't be sure Abram, as he was known at the time, was even a worshiper of Yahweh when God first called him. Abram's first appearance is in a genealogy list at the end of Genesis 11. As chapter 12 opens, God called him to leave everything familiar and go to an unknown place. His willingness to trust God makes him a fit candidate for the roll call of the faithful in Hebrews 11.

But did he really act on blind faith, without even a hint of support or prior understanding? We can't be sure because the Bible is silent on this issue, but I doubt it. I think Abraham had some notion of God, or perhaps he paid attention to the lingering ring of grace God always sounds.

Someone has asked "why did God choose to call Abraham?" The answer is "perhaps because he was the only one listening." God never forces Himself on people. He calls everyone, but the ones who respond have made an effort to listen. Abraham must have been listening, so his faith was not blind at all, but expectant. He knew Someone was there.

People today say they have faced situations that have been far beyond anything they've ever encountered, and had to have faith to step out or to endure a completely new situation. Isn't that blind faith? Not at all. We perhaps often have "marched off the map" of our previous experience, but all the ways God has blessed and guided us in the past prove to be prelude to this new territory we must explore and embrace. That is not blind faith, it is simply our next step in faith.

You may be facing a new and extraordinarily challenging circumstance, but God has used your life to this point to prepare you for this latest expression of His calling. Rather than asking you to act on blind faith, He is simply calling you to act on the evidence and experience at hand. You need to take the next step, but that step is not into total darkness. The light shines behind you enough to give you some notion of where you need to go.

I wouldn't suggest for a moment that the Christian journey comes without any doubt or uncertainty. Belief is not easy. Faith takes muscle, and God certainly doesn't seem ready to show up in the sky. But this reverent uncertainty does not mean that we are left without powerful spiritual and intellectual support! We have evidence, and that evidence comes in several familiar and valuable forms.

Scripture. The Bible is uniquely sacramental in nature, for God communicates to us through it. Its guidance, wisdom, challenge, and comfort are unique and a sure mark of its inspiration. All of the Bible is at least nearly 2000 years old, and parts of it go back another full millennium. The fact that literature so ancient, coming to us through different languages and cultures, addresses so clearly the most important aspects of our lives is singularly remarkable. Genuine spirituality and truth is timeless, and the Bible has proved itself to be a trustworthy guide.

Think about it. We have many different kinds of ancient texts, but no one, that I know of, claims that the Enuma Elish inspires and guides them for life. Homer was brilliant, but neither the Iliad nor the Odyssey changes lives. The Bible does these things. The scripture has a ring of truth that inspires and encourages so that we never face any situation with blind faith.

God's presence. One of the clearest teachings in the scripture, and perhaps its main theme, is that God is with us. We must not ignore or even diminish the vital importance of this truth. Christ abides in you and you in Christ. The Father is with you and will never fail or forsake you. The Holy Spirit whispers comfort to your soul.

We tend to be "practical" today, relying on evidence which can be felt and seen, tested and proved. The problem with the practical approach is that faith is the assurance of things hoped for and the evidence of things not seen. God works quietly, often subtly, not to be evasive, but to drive us to deeper faith in Him. Trusting in God's presence, exploring and cultivating it, therefore, is actually more practical than simply relying on what we can see and touch. The true and deep wonders of God are far beyond what eye can see or ear hear (1 Cor. 2:9).

The fellowship of the faithful. The trials you face are "common to all," and in sharing your struggle with others you open up yourself to help from your brothers and sisters in Christ. You have not walked the difficult path lying before you, but someone you know has, and God has a marvelous way of bringing those people to you.

Frankly, we never lack of direction from God. God is neither silent nor reluctant. In fact, in addition to not believing in blind faith, I also do not believe in unanswered prayers. God is not fickle. He listens and responds because He loves us. His answer may come in the form of an acquaintance who can guide and encourage you. Instead of accusing God of being silent we may need to confess that we are merely obtuse! Someone around you, of a more experienced faith, knows what you are facing and can help you through a hard time. They become God's voice for you.

Without question we see through a glass darkly. Yes, we know in part, but that part means that we need never act with blind faith. God always provides enough light for you to take a step forward. Trust Him. Take the next step.

Reasonably Happy

> *"If you know how to give good gifts to your children, how much more will your Father in heaven give good gifts to those who ask Him?"* Matthew 7:11

Everyone wants to be happy, and that is certainly not a bad thing. I want to be happy. Happiness means my surrounding circumstances are agreeable. Things are going my way. So I'm happy when my health is good, the bills are paid, the Kentucky Wildcats win, etc. I could make a long list of things that make me happy.

The Bible actually has quite a bit to say about happiness. God blesses us in many ways, and some of those ways include health, possessions, and circumstances of all sorts. "He causes the rain to fall on the just and the unjust," Jesus said in the Sermon on the Mount. So God is concerned about our happiness and seems to delight in giving us good things that make for agreeable circumstances.

Of course, this doesn't change the fact that God's major concern is our eternity. So if we spend too much time on trying to be happy, or trying to persuade God to arrange everything to suit us, then we've missed the point entirely. But God enjoys giving us good gifts and encourages us to ask for them. Our happiness is important to God.

But where and how do we draw the line? What can we rightly expect with regard to happiness?

A phrase in the long version of the Serenity Prayer sums up my expectations of happiness. The next to last line reads, "that we may be reasonably happy in this life." That's it. I want to be reasonably happy.

Here are three keys that have helped me.

First, stop trying to be more than reasonably happy. Sure it would be a beautiful morning (and day) if everything's going my way, but is that reasonable? In fact, my expectation that I should have unblemished happiness is one of the impediments to being happy. In some ways, this expectation is vintage American theology. We've come to expect that all discomfort should be eliminated. The fact is, we'd be a lot happier if we settled for being reasonably happy.

An illustration: A few years ago I noticed how many people adamantly said they wouldn't want their children going into the same career they had. I decided to conduct my own survey and began to ask this very question. Rarely would someone say yes. This was true no matter the occupation. Blue collar, white collar, it didn't matter. Now why? Part of the answer surely is that we all believe that something else would make us happier. My survey indicates otherwise. The other person that you might be envying is probably thinking he or she would be a lot happier doing what you're doing.

I decided then that I would aim for 80%. I try to genuinely enjoy 80% of what I do. Every one of my jobs has had about 20% of things that were not very fun, irritating, or even infuriating. But 80% is a B on just about any grading scale. I can be reasonably happy with 80% of things going my way. I'm not really asking you to lower your standards. Just be reasonable. Chances are you'll be quite a bit happier.

Second, accept hardships as the pathway to peace. This is another of my favorite phrases from the Serenity Prayer. The great transformation in the Bible is that suffering actually becomes a means for spiritual growth. This makes it possible for us to shift from trying to change everything to suit us, to looking for spiritual growth that comes with difficulty. Additionally, when viewed in this way, a challenge is not something only to be endured. Amazingly, we find meaning in suffering.

Too many times, at some level, I fear that my life would be nothing but drenching unhappiness if _____ happened. That blank may be a serious health problem personally or with a member of my family. I look at someone else in that feared situation and wonder how they make it. But when I look closer, I often find that they not only are making it but they seem to be filled with deep meaning and purpose. In fact, they appear genuinely, puzzlingly, happy.

I think here of the countless men and women who've been gravely injured serving our country. So often, I see in their lives moving testimonies of how they've met their challenges with greater resolve and thereby found a deeper meaning than they've ever had before.

I've never been a fan of the idea that "everything happens for a reason." I do believe we can construct reason, meaning, and purpose out of any situation. God doesn't bring upon us the storms of life, but neither does He waste them. He gets us through and helps us to find peace, and, yes, happiness. Hardships don't preclude happiness. Faced with faith, they become the means of finding happiness.

Third, stop thinking of happiness and unhappiness as binary. You're never either one or the other. Every life has a bit of both (remember my 80% rule). The line between unhappiness and happiness cuts through us all. When people ask me how I'm doing I often say "I'm reasonably happy." This sometimes provokes a few puzzled looks, but it's accurate because at any given moment I'm a mixture of happiness and unhappiness. Now here is the challenge: I must watch more for the presence of happiness than for its absence. That's not easy!

Unhappiness is like stubbing my little toe. When it happens it's all I think about. I ignore completely the fact that I have 9 other healthy toes, or that I don't have heart disease or cancer, for example. I'm outraged at the unfairness of the universe for putting that table leg right where my little toe was traveling. Any happy life depends on the proper focus. If I look for unhappiness I can find it in the next stubbed toe. But if I look for happiness, I'm surely overwhelmed by it. You always find what you look for in life.

Happiness/unhappiness is very much like the weather. It changes. That's good news because it means that the events leading to my unhappiness almost always dissipate like the storm. Of course, and this is good to remember, it also means that the sunshine is not permanent. I'm learning more and more to simply observe the clouds and the sunshine, accepting their inevitable presence in my life, without attaching any permanent self-evaluation to them. Also, my faith reminds me of the blue skies, or the starry skies, above the clouds. The troubled things of earth will one day give way to the permanence of heaven. And that is a good thought.

Until that eternally happy day, however, we can embrace some fairly simple strategies that will increase our happiness, at least a bit, here and now. Life will throw many hardships at us. We cannot change that any more than we can change the weather. All weather, though, has its purpose and even its glory. I can be happy when I remember that.

God's One Note

"God is love." 1 John 4:8

On my desk is a tuning fork I've had for 25 years or so. This particular tuning fork gives me the note A. It doesn't matter how often I strike it, it will always give me the note A. You can't hear it from a distance. You have to be close. You must listen carefully. I could pack it carefully away and open it up in 20 or 30 years, strike it, and it would give me the note A. Over and over. Always and forever. As long as I listen carefully. This tuning fork gives me the note A.

In his first letter, John wrote very simply that God is love. He didn't write, "God is anger" or "God is wrath" or "God is disgusted" or "God is uninterested." He wrote, "God is love." These four words in Greek, three in English, summarize the fundamental and unchangeable nature of God. Everything God does emanates from love. Everything I know about God must start with love. Love is God's one note.

That's so important to remember because we live in a noisy world, full of discordant notes, and plainly bad ideas about God. We live in a world of anger, wrath, disgust, and apathy. The noise comes from the outside, and too often it comes from a critical voice inside. I know both sources. I also know that when the noise is too loud and too constant I need to pull away to a quiet place and listen for the one note. It's always there, if I'm still enough to hear it. God is love.

John did not always have this idea about God. We have enough information about John to piece together his pilgrimage. We know that Jesus nicknamed him, and his brother James, "Boanerges," a word that means thunder. Sons of thunder. Or as some translators put it sons of commotion or agitation. It was a good nickname, for John, as a young man, was noisy and full of ideas about God that were so noisy and so painful to the ear that it actually risked damaging people around him.

Consider: soon after Jesus first predicted His death, John and James asked Jesus if they could have the places of honor when Jesus fully established His kingdom. They were self-seekers. They had not clearly heard the one note.

Consider: soon after that they came to a Samaritan village, but the people there didn't want anything to do with Jesus. They refused to let Him enter. Two disciples came to him and said, "Lord do you want us to bid fire to come down out of heaven and consume them?" Guess who it was? Two noisy brothers, James and John. You can almost hear the excitement in their voices. Their hatred drove their desire to punish and kill. John had not heard the one note.

At some point, however, perhaps at the cross, he began to hear the note. He came to realize that God was not a God of vengeance and power displays. He had come to die for us because of His great love for us. John heard the one note and realized some things needed to die in him. He got rid of all the noise in the succeeding years and later would write, "God is love." John was transformed by love.

That is the first great truth about God's love that you need to commit to memory. God's love is a transformative energy. It's not just a feeling. It powerfully transforms the life of anyone who accepts it as reality and lives accordingly. It flows into any open heart and changes you from the inside out. God's love transforms.

God's love is the theme of the stories we share with others. We never argue anyone into the kingdom. Or berate them into belief. I do best by simply telling the story of how God's love has changed me. That keeps me from telling other people how they must write their story. I believe that by telling mine, people are more likely to turn to God in a quiet moment and hear the one note.

Sometimes the pain I see in people's lives is nearly overwhelming to me. I mourn for them, hurt for them. They tell me their stories and seem sometimes to be waiting for me to say words that will bring some relief. That's quite a bit of pressure, self-imposed for the most part, and I used to try to find something profound to say that would unlock all the comfort they needed.

For perhaps 40-50 years John listened to that one note until it was the only note he heard. Then he wrote, "God is love." A curious fact about 1 John is that it contains the simplest Greek syntax and vocabulary in the New Testament. The first text a student of Greek translates is usually from John's first letter. I think it's no accident that the simplest language expresses the most profound truth. Keeping it simple results in keeping it clear.

I gave up trying to be profound a long time ago, or rather I stopped trying to manufacture some new insight. I realized that simplicity and depth go hand in hand. I discovered, perhaps like John, that living as if God truly loves me is the best and surest way for me to live with meaning, purpose, and joy. In fact, "God loves you" is the very best assurance I can give a struggler.

Strip away all the noise of the world and we will hear a constant, beautiful note that envelops all of creation. Listen long enough and, wonder of wonders, we discover that God has tuned our hearts to hear and sing that very note.

You're Not the First Person To Do This

"Create in me a clean heart, O God, and put a new and right spirit within me." Psalm 51:10

I have a confession. Not anything nefarious, more along the lines of embarrassingly dumb. One day I wanted to back my prized Ford Taurus about half-way into my garage, and, for reasons too complicated to explain, I hopped out, leaving the door open, *and left the car in reverse.* I'll let that sink in for a moment . . . all right, let's proceed. As I realized the car was still rolling, with its front left "wing" heading slowly toward destruction, I jumped in and jammed on the brake.

Too late. There was an awful, slow, crunching sound. The outer brick wall of my house had bent the door back at a precise 90 degree angle. A car door should stop at about 60 degrees. I sat there for a moment in stunned stupidity. My dear wife, who had witnessed the entire incident, stood in very gracious silence. I pulled forward, and found that while I was still able to close the door, it made a loud popping, grinding sound that said, "This will cost you."

After a few moments of recovery, I sheepishly called my good friend in the car business to ask about arranging for repairs. I explained the situation and repeatedly bemoaned my foolishness. He assured me that they could take care of it, and then he said, "You're not the first person to do this." He had seen situations like this before, and he had fixed every one. I felt better. That line stayed with me: **You're not the first person to do this**, spoken by someone who knew how to fix the problem.

Now let's move from something mildly inane to deeply evil. David's sin is usually remembered as his affair with Bathsheba. The worse sin was trying to deceive Uriah, her husband, into believing he was the father. The sin was unspeakably worse when he arranged for Uriah to be left alone in battle and killed. David took advantage of Uriah's faithfulness and courage to murder him. This sin defies comprehension. Such traitors reside in Dante's ninth and lowest circle of hell.

Nathan the prophet confronted David who quickly confessed and repented. That's all very good, but how do you approach God after such evil?

David wrote Psalm 51 after his encounter with Nathan. He had realized painfully the full impact of what he had done. He described his sin in painful detail. He realized how bad he was. The line quoted for this GraceWaves highlights his plea: "create in me a new heart."

The word *create* (bara in Hebrew) is interesting. The writer of Genesis used it to describe God's activity in the first chapter. "In the beginning, God *created*." Theologians say the word describes creatio ex nihilo, creation out of nothing, but that's not quite accurate. The earth was a formless void when God spoke creation into existence. I like that image better. He took a mess and made beauty.

David confessed to God and held nothing back. He asked Him to create something out of the terrible mess he had made of his life. God did not have much to work with in David, but He doesn't need anything. That's the nature of grace. God creates out of little or even nothing. He cleansed, purified, forgave, and accepted David. How? David was not the first person to do something like that, and God knows how to fix the problem. He is in the business of forgiving and transforming messy people.

I regularly speak with people whose pasts haunt them. They live day to day with a constant burden of self-loathing. For 35 years I looked out over congregations and learned to never underestimate the terrible situations people get themselves into. Some are bearing a crushing guilt and seek to hide from God, certain that if they stood in His presence, openly and honestly, a holy fire would consume them. In Christ, and through His cross, that's not true.

Personally, I depend daily on the depth and richness of God's grace and redemption in my ongoing recovery from alcoholism. I ran headlong into the mess of addiction and the disease welcomed and made a mess out of me. Alcohol drained my spirit. For a time, tt was king in my life. I was desperately lost, not in the sense of salvation. I just don't believe God ever let go of me, but I sure had let go of God. I couldn't stop and then gave up trying. And that is a miserable experience.

I became a Christian when I was nine-years-old. I had not lived a riotous life as an 8-year-old. Redemption, the idea of being rescued, never really personally resonated with me. But when I descended into the hopeless depths of addiction I despaired of life itself. I needed rescuing. Redemption is now very personal to me, and very precious.

The wonderful beauty of grace for me is that when I hit the bottom God was waiting there for me. He didn't watch me fall from above. I think He just walked along beside me until I realized a needed help from a power greater than myself.

Fear keeps us from God. Fear of the past. Fear of the future. Fear of the present. Fear that some action has so offended God that He's forever turned away.

You're not the first person to do this. God knows the very worst about us, but He can create something out of nothing and has been doing this since creation. Each one of us is a new illustration of the original creation, or re-creation. We can give Him our mess. He's seen it all and heard it all. We'll discover not rejection, but a smiling God who was waiting for us all along.

Comfort and Encouragement

"Blessed be the God and Father of our Lord Jesus Christ, the Father of all mercies and God of all encouragement, who comforts us in every affliction so that we may be able to comfort those who suffer affliction with the same encouragement God used to comfort us."
2 Corinthians 1:3-4

Sometimes I need comfort, just someone to love me and reassure me that God will make all things right in His time. Other times I need encouragement, someone to tell me to be courageous, get back up, and keep moving. The Greek language has a single word that has both meanings.

I used comfort and encouragement in the verses above. Both translations are from forms of the same Greek word paraclesis. One nuance of this word is comfort. The Holy Spirit is called the Paraclete in John 14:16 and 26, and the venerable King James Version bequeathed to us the translation of Comforter. It's a good translation. The Holy Spirit is The Comforter. Comfort connotes tender compassion, and we certainly all need God to take us into His arms and comfort us.

The word paraclesis, and its verbal forms, however, also has the meaning of encouragement, exhortation, and beseeching. This nuance means the subject is trying to get the object to do something. It's a call to action.

God's aim is not merely to comfort. He encourages, exhorts, and beseeches us to return to the game, as it were. In fact, Paul's idea here is to receive comfort and encouragement from God so that we may seek out others with whom we share this encouragement. Encouragement has a goal beyond mere comfort, and that is why I prefer that translation. It's something we share.

Paul's letters to the Corinthians reflect both his need for

encouragement and his commitment to encourage. He wrote from personal experience in which he faced discouragement in three main areas: circumstances, vocation, and relationships. These areas of discouragement can threaten to overwhelm any of us. Paul faced each one, and God taught him something important in each one.

<u>Circumstances</u>. Paul wrote of a mysterious but harrowing experience in which he and his companions were so "utterly and unbearably crushed that we despaired of life itself" (2 Cor. 8). We don't have the details, but something happened so traumatic that he felt he had "received the sentence of death."

I know what it's like to despair of life itself, as many of you do. How you emerge on the other side of the events depends on how you receive the grace of God. Paul learned from a tragic circumstance "to rely not on ourselves, but on God who raises the dead" (2 Cor. 1:8-10). God encouraged him. Paul survived and returned to strengthen churches and write letters.

<u>Vocation</u>. In 2 Corinthians 4, Paul wrote about "this treasure" (v. 7), which was his calling and vocation as an apostle. He firmly believed God had called and gifted him to do what he was doing, but he was not always received well. He felt he had failed many times. As a result, he felt "afflicted," "perplexed," "persecuted," and "struck down" (4:8-9). But for each challenge God provided encouragement so that Paul was "not crushed," "not driven to despair," "not forsaken," and "not destroyed." Once again he learned more deeply to rely on the transcendent power that belongs to God (v.7).

<u>Relationships</u>. Betrayal and rejection were consistent themes in Paul's correspondence with the Corinthians. He was not their favorite preacher (1 Cor. 1:12). Some said he could write well but not speak well and that he was not very good looking! (2 Cor. 10:10). Others claimed he was not a "real apostle" and thus inferior (2 Cor. 11:5). I could cite many other passages. Paul had a very rough time with people he loved and depended on. People he counted on disappointed him, but in these weak moments of despair he learned

that God's grace is perfected in weakness (2 Cor. 12:9).

Most of us can relate to every area of discouragement cited. We might be in the middle of a difficult time in which we don't see a way forward, or have lost a job, or have needless struggles with people we thought we could trust and rely on.

God is with you. He will give you the comfort you need, but He also exhorts you to keep pushing ahead and use your gifts and opportunities.

When Gregory was about 5, I was putting decking in our attic. Of course, he wanted to help nail, so I set a few nails for him to work on while I continued in another area. Squatting down and swinging the hammer with two hands, he was making steady progress every third strike or so. On one backswing, however, he hit his forehead with the back of the hammer. He dropped it and ran to me, burying his face in my chest, crying, and rubbing the small bump forming right above his eyes.

I hugged him and told him I had hit various parts of my body on countless occasions. As I continued to console him, he pushed away from me, went back and picked up the hammer, and finished driving the nail. He then came back to my embrace, again rubbing his head, and said, "I wasn't going to quit." I love that!

Comfort helps us to feel better. Encouragement helps us to do better. While God certainly does want to comfort us, I believe His main goal is to encourage us to re-enter the fray. The affliction we face is common to all people, and God is with us to strengthen and console. But He also wants us to get back to life. We have His encouragement. Now we can encourage someone else.

Thin Places
(An Advent GraceWaves)

"Set your minds, therefore, on things that are above, not on things of the earth." Colossians 3:2

Many years ago, I ran across a concept in Celtic theology called "thin places." It's the idea that certain places are sacred, and that in those places the distance between our physical world and the spiritual world is quite thin. The sacred places offer us the opportunity to look beyond the surrounding clamor of empty busyness and "see" what is true, real, and eternal. Thin places nurture our souls.

I'd like to expand the idea of the thin places to include thin times. The principle is still the same. Though the physical world is most obvious, it is the spiritual world with its values and relationships that feeds our true hunger. We need times, both regular and spontaneous, that call us to transcendence. That's especially important in a grating culture that ignores the sacred.

Thin places may be a sanctuary, chapel, forest, or a place in your home. Jesus retreated often to the wilderness, or a lonely place, after a long time with crowds and their demands. Thin times include daily prayer, meditation, and contemplation, a weekly Sabbath, and other annual holy days such as Easter and Advent.

Advent is perhaps the most obvious candidate for being a thin time, but also the most vulnerable to being completely neglected. The irony is thick. As we celebrate the event when the space between heaven and earth was at its thinnest, we're likely to be more overwhelmed and spiritually undernourished than perhaps any other time of the year.

Survey the crowds in the malls or in traffic and you likely will detect a soul-weariness. Yes, nearly everyone is caught up in Christmas, but apparently no one is happy about it. CNN annually runs a story about tempers flaring at Black Friday events, and in more recent years we have the blessing of accompanying video. Charming.

But you don't have to immerse yourself in the hoards to experience the emptiness. All of the great spiritual leaders for thousands of years have pointed out our fundamental spiritual need. The Law, Prophets, and Writings all point to God as the sole answer to our spiritual craving. Jesus used metaphors like water and bread to describe Himself as our essential spiritual sustenance. Paul contrasted the spirit and flesh and exhorted us to fix our eyes on things above, not things below.

The first noble truth in Buddhism is usually translated as "life is suffering," but in my reading it seems a better translation to say that life is longing. We all know something is missing, something is not quite right, and no amount of what the world offers will fill that fundamental emptiness. The unfilled spiritual vacuum is at the heart of all our anxiety, anger, addictions, and acquisitiveness.

Advent offers a special challenge and opportunity. This is a busy time of year, and we usually spend more money than we should buying presents for people who have absolutely everything they need and just about everything they could reasonably want. This season is marked by a garish noise, and the thin places and times get pushed to the background or forgotten altogether.

The fundamental challenge lies at this very point: the world shouts, but God whispers. Our salvation lies in recovering and cherishing the thin places and thin times.

This recovery does not mean entering a monastery from late November to the first of the new year. If we can't catch our spiritual breath in the middle of life then we really don't stand much of a chance of surviving anyway.

What we need is a spiritual and mental shift that allows us to become aware of God around us and in us all of the time. When you go to church, be there. Allow yourself the luxury of singing the hymns, saying the prayers, and listening to the sermon as if in each part of worship God is trying to speak directly to you. He is! The worship service, or hanging of the green, or Christmas Eve can be a thin place if you're simply present and not mentally wrestling with the list of unmet and usually unrealistic demands.

This shift truly can make a tremendous difference. The lights remind you of the Light that dispels darkness. Presents remind you of the true Gift. Decorations remind you of beauty. Advent is full of symbols. Taking time to remember their significance helps you make the shift.

Most importantly, we simply must make time to be still. Usually that means physically being still so that we become aware of the spiritual world. It's hard to breathe deeply of things that are spiritual if we're huffing and puffing our way through every hour. However, being still can also mean taking a few moments to say a prayer of awareness in the midst of the busyness. I believe God loves this kind of prayer. The clamor of the world does not silence God. It simply means we have to be intentional in listening for the ways God speaks, and He's always speaking.

A scene from Bernard Shaw's St. Joan illustrates my point. St. Joan claims to hear the voice of God, and with that conviction she inspires men to follow her. The prince, however, is jealous. "Why don't the voices come to me? I am king not you!" he whines. Joan answers, "They do come to you, but you do not hear them. As soon as the angelus rings you cross yourself and have done with it. But if you prayed from your heart and sat in the field and listened for the trilling of the bells after they stopped ringing, then you would hear the voices just as I."

Real spirituality is simply a matter of being aware, and we have the opportunity right now. Advent is here. The bells are ringing, and God is whispering. Where are your thin places? What are your thin times?

Complainers

"To what shall I compare this generation? They are like children sitting in the market place and calling to one another 'We piped to you, and you did not dance; we wailed, and you did not weep!" Luke 7:31-32

This is an odd parable. You're likely to have overlooked it all of your Bible-reading life. You may recall it vaguely, but have you have really stopped to think about why Jesus told it? By the way, I think Jesus told it with a slight smile on His face.

Here's the context. Though popular with the people because of His teaching and miracles, the Pharisees and lawyers murmured their complaints in the background. Jesus did not fit into their plans, and they would gripe to anyone who would listen.

Jesus knew what was going on, and He knew also that their criticisms would spread and become shouts to crucify Him. So He told an unusual parable to describe complainers. He looked around and saw children playing in the village square. And what kind of games did they play?

A wedding was the biggest social celebration in a village. It was a community event in which the entire village would participate. The wedding took place outdoors. The procession went through the streets. The newly-married bride was lifted above the crowd and paraded around. They played music and danced. Can't you imagine children in that day would want to play wedding? "Let's play wedding!"

But there were complainers in the crowd of kids. "No, we don't want to play wedding." So the other children would say, "We played the pipes but you don't want to dance!"

All right. If not wedding how about funeral? A funeral was another big social occasion. Children had seen funerals, and I imagine they might reenact one. Or perhaps it was like in my family. I have performed good Christian funerals for three dogs, two parakeets, a cat, and some fish. Jesus had seen some children imitating the adults in all the pomp and circumstance.

But the complainers again objected, "No, we don't want to play that either." And so the others would say, "We wailed and you did not weep."

Then Jesus brings home the meaning (Luke 7:33-35). God had acted in history during this time in a remarkable way. John the Baptist entered the world with a message of a rough-hewn prophet. In camel's hair and leather girdle, full of locusts and wild honey he said, "Repent or the judgment of God will fall upon you!" He was not always accepted, but he was never vague. Many listened, most rejected him.

Then came Jesus. The Messiah Himself arrived, and He was different from His cousin. John the Baptist went out into the wilderness and never took a course in how to win friends and influence people. Jesus was completely opposite. He intentionally traveled through villages and towns. He liked being around people, went to their weddings, their funerals, their feasts. He would sit up late talking and loved the crowds.

What did people say about Him? A few loved Him, but many more rejected Him. What was Jesus' verdict? "John the Baptist comes with judgment and you say he has a demon. I come with grace and you say I eat and drink too much." Some people in that day could not be satisfied.

And people today have the same habit. **Nothing is satisfying**. We live in a culture of complaint where the reigning goal is to highlight unhappiness. Desperately trying to find something to satisfy us even for a short period of time, we settle into a pattern of always wanting what we do not have and forever shifting the target for happiness.
Ours is the most marketed-to generation in the history of the world. Researchers know what a 59-year-old man like me wants. When I click on CNN they know my surfing tendencies. I go to

Amazon.com and it says, "Welcome Terry" and they have recommendations for me to purchase. I go to Wal-Mart and the entire store is designed to make me purchase as much as possible at low, low prices.

What our society has produced is self-focus on steroids. We have wonders available to satisfy our latest need without realizing our need has been created by advertisers and marketers. Whatever you want, you can have at a dozen stores or delivered via on-line within a few days. We expect the self to be happy, and when the self is not happy we complain, become easily offended, fix the blame on someone else, and completely overlook God.

Surely one of the worst sins in life is failing to see what God is doing around and in you. He really is always at work, and He really does love and care for you. To neglect to look around and see His presence and blessing is surely a form of the original sin.

Thomas Merton wrote, "To be grateful is to recognize the love of God in everything He has given us--and He has given us everything. Every breath we draw is a gift of His love, every moment of existence is a grace, for it brings with it immense graces from Him. Gratitude, therefore, takes nothing for granted, is never unresponsive, is constantly awakening to new wonder and to praise the goodness of God. For the grateful person knows that God is good, not by hearsay but by experience. And that is what makes all the difference."*

Discernment leads to gratitude, and gratitude silences complaint. God has acted in history, and He acts today. We can be still for a moment, draw back from the keening cries of want and dissatisfaction, and remember that God has anticipated and taken care of our every need. The awareness of such abundance silences complaint.

*<u>Thoughts in Solitude</u>, p. 43, 1956. Copyright by The Abbey of Our Lady of Gethsemani. Published by Farrar, Strauss and Giroux, NY.

Scabs or Scars?

> *"Mary, called Magdalene, from whom seven demons had gone out."* Luke 8:2

On my left knee I have a two-inch scar courtesy of a circular saw back in 1981. When I first cut myself, it was not a scar at all, of course. It was a bleeding, open wound that soaked my jeans and sock. At Barbourville (KY) General Hospital a nurse cleaned it out, stopped the bleeding, and a doctor stitched it closed. The scab formed and eventually fell off leaving a white scar on my sun-starved white leg.

We all have scars and stories to share of how we got them. Scars are physical markers of hurt. The scars on our bodies are reminders of the pain we felt. We suffered, and the scar is proof.

Injuries that scar the soul hurt more.

Mary Magdalene had her share of those scars. Seven of them. They were called demons, and in that day any malady could be attributed to a demon. So in addition to some real demons, she probably also suffered from some physical ailments and possibly some mental illness. We don't know much about her (the woman in Luke 7:37ff is never identified as Mary in the scripture), but we can well imagine that she had a very difficult life, suffered a lot of pain, and probably inflicted her share of it on other people.

When she met Jesus she was full of wounds, and the psychic ones were the worst. The pain of the mind and soul is the most jagged and is the source of the pain we bring to others. Many of Mary's wounds were fresh, some had scabbed over, but none had truly healed. Then Jesus healed her, and she began to follow Him all the way to the cross and became the first preacher of the gospel of the resurrection. The scabs had turned into scars, and how beautiful those scars were!

Now take a look at your soul wounds. We all have them. Are they scabs? Or are they scars? What role do we have in moving from one to the other?

The key is to stop picking at the scab. Each wound is real, but rehearsing the cause, remembering the person responsible for the wound, and showing everyone the gash just prolongs the bleeding and the pain.

Ever hear of the woman who complained so much about her husband you'd think he was still alive?

Fresh wounds take some time for the healing to begin. But too often I've noticed that most of us keep picking at old wounds so that the healing never progresses. We feel resentment at the person who hurt us, or we feel guilt and shame for how we hurt others. We endlessly rehearse how we got the wound and ensure the scab never becomes a scar.

The past can hurt us today, in some degree, to the extent we allow it. Mary carried the scars of her past for the rest of her life, but she was not bound by her wounds, self-inflicted or otherwise. God offers grace to move on. It can be grace to forgive or grace to feel forgiven or grace to let go. Grace is what we need to begin turning the scab into a scar.

Of course, God clearly has a role in our healing. Despite what some people preach, God is simply not in the business of bringing pain into our lives. Jesus never hurt anyone, never brought a disease on anyone, and certainly never killed anyone. He said, "If you have seen Me you have seen the Father" (John 14:9). Watching Jesus shows us what God is like. God is not interested in hurting us. He longs to heal us.

Our tendency when hurt is to ask why, and the chief "why" question is "Why did God do this?" Here's the answer: He didn't. We live in a broken world. It affects and afflicts us all through disease, accidents, death, and injustice. Sometimes the pain comes through our own terrible choices. Either way we are better off to deal with life as life is. God doesn't mind the questions, but think about it. If we knew the answer to any "why" question, would that really relieve the pain? Probably not. The wound would still be there.

The truth is God's blessings often come to us in mysterious ways, and sometimes the blessing is cloaked initially in pain and trouble. Give God some time and trust. We throw up our hands and say "all is lost!" God responds with a smile and says, "Of course it's not! The story just isn't finished yet."

Mary came to Jesus. In the same way we can bring Him our wounds. We just need to stop arguing about it and let Him start the healing. He can transform the scab into a glorious scar. Countless people now speak of the most difficult times in their lives as occasions when God demonstrated His power through their weakness. They're just showing off their scars!

So lets look again at the pain we're feeling today. We have a right to hurt, but we also have a need to heal. Are we picking at the wound? Or has the healing started? The Great Physician waits patiently.

Change Your Mind, Change Your Life

"Do not be conformed to this world, but be transformed by the renewal of your mind." Romans 12:2

What are you thinking about right now? I'm flattered if you say you've devoted your full concentration to this devotional, but I want you to consider what your mind drifts to when in neutral. In other words, when you're engaged in a task that requires no mental effort, like mowing the grass or dusting furniture, what do you think about?

Honestly, my mind often gravitates to negative experiences, perhaps a personal conflict or disappointment. Without realizing it, or without consciously choosing the topic, I can find myself in a mental court of appeals thinking about what I should have said or should have done in a particular event. My hurt, anger, resentment, disappointment, and fear often bubbles to the surface, and I suddenly realize that for perhaps the last fifteen minutes I have been mentally wrestling with something or someone. I'm not alone in this kind of experience.

Psychologists call it "rumination," the obsession and over-thinking of a life event. It magnifies or perhaps is even a chief cause of a host of psychological problems (e.g. anxiety, depression, and PTSD) and negative behaviors (e.g. binge drinking or eating). Brain scans reveal that consistent negative thoughts and emotions have a tremendous effect on the brain and the neural circuitry that shapes our perception of ourselves and the world. What you think about matters enormously.

The mind, it seems, is a battlefield, where we must fight to think of things spiritual. This fact is constantly recognized throughout the scripture. Meditation is well-represented in the psalms. Psalm 1 sets the tone for the entire psalter, and its opening exhortation is to mediate on the law of the Lord. Psalm 119, the lengthiest chapter in the Bible, is essentially an encouragement to think about the goodness of God's laws.

The Bible in many ways charts the movement from an early emphasis on external behaviors (Leviticus) to the inner life of meditation and motive in the New Testament. The highpoint of Jeremiah's prophecy is God's promise to not only put His law in the hearts of His people but *to be known* by them, from the least to the greatest. God desires not a second-hand acquaintance, but a deeply personal relationship.

In the New Testament, with its intermingling of Greek concepts, we see not only the fulfillment of this prophecy but an intensified focus on the mind. Perhaps most significantly is Jesus' version of the ancient Shema and His addition of loving God "with all your mind." That's not in Deuteronomy, but it is on the lips of Jesus in all three of the Synoptic Gospels.

Paul, with his deep Greek roots, had a great deal to say about the mind. When we add his references to "the heart" and "the *psuche*" (soul or life) as the origin of our thinking the evidence mounts. The Romans 12 passage above is perhaps his clearest reference to the Christian mandate to have a transformed and renewed mind in order to experience God.

Notice the passive voice of "be transformed." Paul did not say "transform yourself." He recognized that this renewal is a work of God, far beyond our strength and ability. My thinking that often gets me in trouble is not sufficient to get me out of trouble. I need help, and God genuinely delights in stepping in and making this transformation.

But of course, God, in my understanding, doesn't do much of anything to us without our consent and cooperation. Prayer and meditation have a vital role in clearing up and strengthening my mind. I must practice good neural hygiene, and I can do that by consciously challenging my old mind's tendency to ruminate when I'm mowing the grass! Better still to develop some good practices before I fire up the mower.

What the Bible has given us poetically or intuitively, science confirms prosaically. Modern brain scans (over the last 20 years or so) have led to a whole new area of study called neuro-theology. That's just one of the coolest terms I've run across lately. It's the idea that we strengthen areas of our brain based on our prayers and meditations. Certain areas of our brains (areas associated with higher functions) "light up" in scans of praying and meditating priests and nuns. Coincidentally, the areas associated with fear and anger cool down.

Very practically, this means that you can change your brain by careful attention to spiritual practices. What you focus on makes a difference in the way you think and consequently how you feel.

In his book, Spiritual Evolution, Harvard psychiatrist George Vaillant writes of the importance of positive emotions such as love, joy, faith, awe, gratitude, and others. These emotions are part of our genetic wiring. These are also a common denominator of all major faiths. Any Christian is bound to recognize in Vaillant's list the echoes of the fruit of the Spirit (Gal. 5:22-23).

God has put within my grasp the means to having a more pleasant grass-mowing experience. Whenever I'm assailed by the negative emotions of fear, anger, resentment, etc., I can make a conscious commitment to focusing on love, joy, peace, patience, kindness, goodness, faithfulness, gentleness, and self-control. This focus must be gentle, not a angry mental wrestling match. I must also intentionally set aside times to pray and meditate in the quiet watches of the night or early morning.

An analogy: if you were concerned about the weakness of your biceps, a physical therapist might tell you that if you did curls with a small dumbbell in three sets of 10, both sides, once a day, your arm will inevitably strengthen. It's a physiological certainty.

I can assure you, based not only on scripture but also on the latest developments of neuroscience, that a consistent life of prayer and meditation, perhaps 12 minutes a day, will inevitably strengthen the "spiritual" areas of your brain. It will change your mind, and give you an entirely different outlook on life, your problems, your joys, your highs, your lows. It's a spiritual certainty.

Find or write prayers (it's not that hard) that highlight gratitude, trust, joy, compassion, and forgiveness. The Prayer of St. Francis is a wonderful example. Pray them. Say uplifting passages of scripture repeatedly. These practices tune your mind to God.

With all the negative emotions flooding us regularly, we desperately need a spiritual revival to turn the tide. Begin with you. Think about, meditate on, and pray to the God of grace, peace, and love. Your will life will be transformed.

Grace for When You're Not Totally Depraved

"What are you doing here Elijah?" 1 Kings 19:9

Driving to church one morning I thought about the thousands of people I passed in their homes or cars. What were they like spiritually? I decided, accurately I think, that very few of them are murderers, serial adulterers, chronically undependable, lying, cheating scoundrels. Most people are probably muddling their way through life with occasional episodes of low level road hostility (not full-blown road rage), fudging on taxes, and padding résumés.

Now I'm not letting all the more respectable sinners off the hook. We can avoid all of the big, ugly, public sins, and still be a spiritual mess, of course. We're pretty good at keeping our badness private or minimizing it so we can sleep at night.

It's good to remember that it takes very little to have to declare spiritual bankruptcy. We can't buy holiness or work our way into heaven. We all have a debt that is unpayable with our meager resources. Thank God for grace! Comparing ourselves to one another and patting ourselves on the back for being at least a little better than the other guy is a total waste of time and actually does a good bit of spiritual harm. When it comes to comparing and rating ourselves I like a quote attributed to Dolly Parton who, when pressed about numerous rumors of her indiscretions, finally said "Hell, I've either done it or I'm capable of it."

Trust me, I've done it or I'm capable of it.

My reason for spending a little bit of space leveling the ground, so to speak, is that when it comes to grace we usually talk about how God's grace extends to the very worst of sinners. That's true. But again most of you reading this are not "murderers, serial adulterers, chronically undependable, lying, cheating scoundrels." Grace is wonderful for the front page failures some of us have, but it's also essential for the back page details. Grace works for the spiritual paper cuts and the severed jugular.

Let's take Elijah as an example. He was a man of powerful faith, no capital S sins.

The most familiar and impressive scene in his story is the contest with the prophets of Baal. To prove who had the stronger God, Elijah set up a "burnt offering contest." Build two altars, and see which God shows up with fire.

Elijah was at his faithful, trash-talking best. Literally. The altars were set up. The contest started, and the prophets of Baal began their dancing and futile pleading. When nothing happened Elijah mocked them saying "Maybe he's deep in thought, or gone to the bathroom (that's a likely meaning of the Hebrew), taken a trip, or taking a nap." Of course, nothing happened though the prophets cut themselves and continued their rave.

Then it was Elijah's turn. He laid out the wood and then in a final theatrical flourish had servants douse the burnt offering with water. Three times. The wood and the animal were drenched and water filled a trench Elijah dug around the altar. Then he prayed, and fire came down from heaven and consumed "the animal, the wood, the stones, the dust, and the water in the trench." (1 Kings 18:20-40).

This is a great biblical story with a dash of Vince McMahon. Elijah won the day, slew the prophets (which is what they did in those less tolerant days), was greatly acclaimed, and lauded by the king. This was his high point.

And in the next chapter he comes off looking kind of like a wilted flower. Queen Jezebel, who was a fan of Baal, promised to kill him. He ran for his life into the wilderness. He felt like a failure: "I am no better than my fathers," and wished for death.

Think about this. He had just set up and witnessed a stunning demonstration of God's presence and power. Yet now his heart melted because of some threats.

The next scene is very memorable, for God caused a strong wind to break the rocks in front of Elijah's cave, then an earthquake to rattle the land, then a fire to blaze through the valley. Then the still, small voice of God.

Elijah's reaction? The same. He tells God he's a failure and no one listens, and he's the only faithful man left in the land and everyone is trying to kill him. God's reaction? "I've got 7000 worshipers still, and you need to get back to work" (1 Kings 19:15-18).

I've spent quite a bit of space with this story because I want us to see the contrast. Elijah's lowest point spiritually came soon after his highest point. Elijah was not a vulgar sinner reeling drunkenly down the middle of the road. But while he was not a capital S sinner, he sure was capable of some capital S self-pity. And God had grace for that, too. God never abandoned him or even appeared to lose patience. God just kept being God, no matter what mood Elijah was in or what struggle he went through.

God's grace is for my self-centered, ugly worst and for my elegant best and for the times when I'm just slogging through life with a kind of dull faith. God's with me when I'm at my best, my very worst, or when I'm just kind of grumpy and full of low-level complaints.

I need grace not only to build the walls and foundations of my life, but to fill in the cracks. I need grace to get into heaven, but I also need grace to give me a little bit of heaven moment by moment. I need grace when I'm really, really bad, and I need grace when I'm just in a bad mood. I need grace when I'm a wretch, and I need grace when I'm just having a bad day. I need grace when I'm totally depraved, and I need grace when I'm just a little rotten. God lovingly offers grace for both polarities, every point in between, and every moment and mood.

Help!

"Religion that is pure and undefiled before God the Father is this: to visit orphans and widows in their affliction."
James 1:27

Help. When you read that word what comes to mind? Do you see it as a request or an imperative? Is it "Help me!"? Or "Help someone!"?

Both are essential.

"Help me" is a frank admission that we can't make make it through life in our own strength. We all need help, and asking for help actually comes quite naturally to us very early in life. My granddaughter regularly asks for help, whether it's carrying a chair to set up a tea party, reading a book, or cutting up her food. She needs help. She asks. She gets help. Wonderful!

As we grow, however, that simple little progression gets more complicated. Somewhere along the line we stop asking for help because it's often seen as a sign of weakness. We want to project strength and independence. "Help? I don't need help!" Sometimes the answer is a little more benign, as in "I don't want to bother anyone else."

It took me a very long time to see the folly of that approach in my own life. I was not good at asking for help, basically for the reasons I cited in the previous paragraph. People asked me for help, but I didn't regularly seek out the help of others.

Frankly, that was an expression of raw pride, the kind of original sin that is the foundation of all the others. Not asking for help wore me out and nearly destroyed me. My personal recovery from alcoholism chiefly involved accepting the fact that I needed help.

Today I ask for help. When I'm afraid, angry, hurt, doubtful, or uncertain I talk to someone else. Wonder of wonders, I've discovered the voice of God through the people I talk to! God doesn't make a habit of speaking to me as He did to Moses, but He's no less talkative. I just needed to learn to listen in the way He normally speaks. I believe God does speak directly to me, but I know my ego speaks to me in my own voice, and it's hard to tell the difference sometimes. God speaks most clearly to me through the voices of others.

You don't have to have an addiction to experience the painful isolation of not asking for help, and the refusal to ask for help is always spiritually dangerous. Ironically, "I need help" *is* a sign of weakness. The scripture consistently challenges us to admit our weakness, not to shame us but to open us up to God's strength. The greatest paradox, of course, is that our weakness becomes the single most important place God demonstrates His power. Go ahead and ask for help.

"Help someone" means that we are looking beyond ourselves to the needs of another person. I say this reverently, but confidently: we shift from listening for God's voice to *being* God's voice. It's vital to ask for help, and it's vital to help someone else.

If we only ask for help we risk becoming what we fear; chronic victims, wallowing in self-pity. God does strengthen and encourage and guide and carry us along in an infinite variety of ways, but He also expects us to serve one another. As the passage from James suggests, good religion consists of simple acts of service like helping orphans and widows. Jesus summed up His ministry as one of serving others. The second greatest commandment is that we love one another. How is love expressed best? By helping one another, of course.

This outward focus brings an almost luminous quality to life. Think back to a time when you helped someone. It can be an endless variety of things: an encouraging word, visiting someone in the hospital, mowing the lawn of an elderly neighbor, etc. How did you feel when you helped? I suggest that feeling of satisfaction and spiritual warmth is very god-like. You felt what God did at creation, "this is *good*."

The wondrous variety of help needed around us means that your day is full of potential *good*. Just start watching for opportunities. Nothing will make us feel more a part of God's powerful providence than helping someone.

A part of my morning prayer in recent years is "Guide me to someone I can help, and grant that I may watch and listen for those You send to help me." I commend this prayer to you. Just say "Help!" It works both ways. Then become aware of the moments each day when God speaks to you, and you speak for God.

The Case of the Unwashed Hands

"I will remember their sins and their misdeeds no more." Hebrews 10:17

All preachers are grateful for their children, if for no other reason than that they are little walking bundles of sermon illustrations. Of course, as children get older they tend to resent even the subtlest hint that they are related to the preacher. I tried to respect the privacy of my own two, except when it was late on Saturday night and I was desperate.

I did broach the subject with my daughter Lauren when she was about 4. We were on the way home from church, and I had mentioned her in the sermon that morning. I asked if that bothered her. She said it did not. I then very sincerely told her that there would likely come a day when it did and not to hesitate letting me know. Clearly trying to reassure me she said, "It's all right, Daddy. I'm usually asleep by then anyway."

Which brings me to my granddaughter, who, as of this writing, is three and about to be the centerpiece of this brief devotional. One day she too will become an eye-rolling teen and forbid public mention of anything about her life. I will respect that, but right now she can't read and is totally fair game.

The incident in question regards handwashing. I hasten to add here at the outset that handwashing is filled with religious significance especially among our Jewish forbearers. It's no small matter. The following story is fraught with deep religious overtones.

Not really. The handwashing in this case was nothing nearly so serious. We were at the supper table, Emily Grace had to use the potty, and upon her return Leslie (Mamère) asked if she had washed her hands. She hesitated in such a way that clearly indicated she had not. Again this was no big deal, and one of the great things about being a grandparent is that you don't tend to view every little incident as predictive of either future success or a life of crime and dissolution.

When asked, "Are you sure you washed your hands?" she nodded but started to look exceedingly guilty and tear up. At this point, I sensed a theological application coming. I suggested we just go back into the bathroom and do a good hand wash. Interestingly, she had closed the bathroom door (covering up her sin!).

Poor little thing looked absolutely miserable. Again, neither Leslie nor I had raised our voices or even sounded doubtful or accusing. We had just asked simple questions. But something was bothering her. She knew that she had crossed a line with people she loved.

Now as her Gandy I had a decision to make. Should I descend upon her with thundering clouds of judgment and accusation? Or should I take a gentler approach? Relax. I chose the latter.

I knelt down and said, "You're not in trouble. Gandy loves you. If you want to tell me something, you can. It's ok." Now if she had tearfully confessed, then this would have been THE PERFECT ILLUSTRATION. But she did not. She just kind of melted into my arms and cried.

It's still a good story though, with roots that go all the way back to Eden.

I did not threaten or punish her. She was doing that all by herself. I kept reassuring her that she could tell me whatever was bothering her, and that she would feel better if she did. She's just not there yet. One day I'm sure she'll understand.

One of the great misconceptions about God is that He is the slinger of lightning bolts, or, as J. B. Phillips put it, the resident policeman. Too many folks believe He's got His finger hovering over the "smite button," just waiting for us to step out of line.

You can certainly point to a lot of biblical texts if you want to take that position, most all of them in the raw Old Testament. But the Bible is not flat. It has a progression to it, and in the latter days we've seen God clearly through His Son. The fact of the matter is Jesus never punished a sinner. Not once. He had harsh words for the hyper-religious people who were keen to punish sins, but He was known as a friend of sinners. That's so powerfully significant, yet so often overlooked.

I know some people point to the second coming as the time when Jesus will get even, but they don't have to be so gleeful about it. Besides, let's handle the apocalyptic texts with care. Being literal in Revelation is a little dicey. But that's another subject, and I'll deal with the emails I'll be getting for this little excursus.

The point here, and the one illustrated by my granddaughter, is that we're not so much punished for our sins as by our sins. I remember them and suffer for them long after God has dismissed them. Sure God hates sin, but He hates it because it hurts His children. His driving purpose is to remove sin, guilt, shame, and restore us to joy. My heart ached for Emily Grace and her tender conscience. I longed for nothing more than to relieve her burden. I think that's the way God responds to my transgressions.

Raphael Simon put it this way, "God can exercise his mercy when we avow our defects. Our defects acknowledged, instead of repelling God, draw him to us, satisfying his longing to be merciful. As this is understood through meditation, the person realizes that those things by which he feels unlovable are exactly what he has to offer God to attract him."*

So Emily Grace was not ready yet to "avow her defects." She'll be fine. I need to be ready to avow mine before God and know that I really will feel so much better when I do. It doesn't make me a bad person to have those defects. It makes me human. And I am one of the humans God longs to shed His mercy upon, to take into His arms, and to assure me that I am still His.

---

*Raphael Simon, "The Spiritual Program—Its Importance for Mental Health," *Studies in Formative Spirituality*, 10:2 (May 1989), p. 163.

Signposts, Not Signs

"Blessed are those who have not seen, yet believe." John 20:29

Have you ever taken a leap of faith? The "leap of faith" is a commonly used phrase to describe the final act of a person to believe that a particular direction is in keeping with God's will. It apparently dates back to Kierkegaard, who actually wrote "leap *to* faith." The phrase was his description of the final act of will to embrace the paradoxes of the Christian faith.

In other words, you take a leap of faith when the commitment seems unlikely, un-provable, or counter-intuitive. We come to the end of a process of analysis and find a cliff. Something does not make sense. At that point, you embrace faith and make the leap.

Now have you ever made a leap of faith? I have to say, I can't think of a time when I have. That may surprise you, but after hearing the phrase a number of times in different contexts, I believe it is overused and misapplied. Let me explain.

To say that we often must make a leap of faith implies that God has left a great chasm between you and the truth or direction you seek. But is that the case? Not at all. Yes, some aspects of the Christian life require tremendous trust and commitment, but I don't find any of the Christian life or faith to be lacking considerable empirical support.

Even at the beginning of faith, when a person first commits to Christ, that act is not really a leap against all logic and evidence. When faced squarely, sin has made a mess of our lives, we cannot adequately "forgive ourselves," and communion with a holy and perfect God is beyond our ability. Those few bits of rational evidence lead me to believe that we do need a Savior, and if I survey history there was one Man who lived a sinless life, assured us of a good and loving God, and offered forgiveness through His death. Then, of course, we have the empirical evidence of His resurrection.

Are we really left at that point with a giant chasm that defies reason? Not at all. So the leap of faith may not really be a leap at all, just a step toward God in which we move away from self and into His embrace.

Now I do not want to quibble with the phrase when used on the grand scale of salvation, but I do want to object to its rather common use to describe many decisions and commitments we make as Christians. Staying faithful to your spouse is not a leap of faith. Neither is attending church, or tithing, or acting with integrity in your business. Forsaking gossip is not a leap of faith. Living graciously and showing kindness does not require a leap of faith.

There are many times when we must take *a step of faith* that brings us closer to God's will in our lives, but even at that point God has given us tremendous encouragement and proof. For example, remember the power of scripture: "the word of our God will stand forever" (Isa. 40:8), and "the word of God is living and active" (Heb. 12). If a particular direction is in keeping with the principles we find in God's word, then you do not need to make a leap of faith. Or pay attention to the counsel of trusted Christian friends. God often speaks through His servants to His servants (Prov. 15:22). I rely heavily on grace-filled brothers and sisters in Christ to offer wise counsel.

Too often we are like the rich man in Luke 16 who, after his death, begged Abraham to send Lazarus to his family to warn them. Abraham's response is that God already had provided sufficient direction. Signs would not help when faith is required. We may want signs, but God provide signposts. In fact, I find these all around me, showing me the directions I must go.

There is an old story about a man lost in high foggy mountains, slipping over an edge and then clinging for his life to a ledge. He calls desperately for help, and voice came to him: "I live on these mountains, and I know exactly where you are. I am across a chasm and cannot get to you, but you must trust me. There is another ledge directly beneath you that will lead you to safety. Just let go and you will drop about a foot. You will be safe."

Last year I wrestled with a decision about leaving a career I had invested more than 30 years in to start a new direction. Many voices encouraged me to take that step. My sense of God's Spirit within told me that it was right. God had placed many signposts around me. Yet, I clung to the ledge. Finally, I let go. I have found, not a chasm of uncertainty and threat, but a smiling God who has welcomed me on a new path. I just had to let go. I launched Chrysalis Interventions (chrysalisinterventions.com) and am so very grateful that God gave me the courage to take the step. I've found solid footing only when I was willing to take the step.

So I prefer the phrase "a step of faith" to "a leap of faith" because I simply do not think that God often requires us to do something that is utter nonsense. We use the spiritual gifts of discernment, wisdom, knowledge, and, yes, faith to submit one other area of our lives more deeply to God's will and purpose. We do not wait for signs of what we should do. Jesus discouraged this. But look for the signposts. They're usually sufficiently clear. When we follow them, we move step by step into the joy for which our God created us.

Resentments

"Let all bitterness, and wrath and anger and slander and malice be put away from you." Ephesians 4:31

We can carry around a lot of heavy emotional and spiritual burdens, and Paul listed some of them in this verse. While a word study would be helpful, let's summarize these four emotions/actions under the banner of "resentments."

I heard someone recently say that every slight, insult, or angry word aimed at us is like a stone. Most people take the stones and put them in a backpack, carrying them around day after day. The backpack gets heavier and heavier, and we don't realize the burden we're carrying. Sound accurate?

To illustrate the problem I have in this area, my first reaction on hearing this analogy was to think that I could hunt down the offender, throw all the rocks back at him or her, and walk away lighter. The Bible has a better way, and I obviously have some work to do.

We first must agree with Paul that we have resentments. Assuming that every resentment is permanently dealt with and put away is hazardous. They can linger for years and darken our days. They are like a forest fire. You can put out the flames, but the fire still smolders in the roots. I've heard that the fire can slowly burn for some distance and erupt in another place, sometimes after days or weeks.

We can't fully put away something we've simply ignored. We should ask God's help in discerning the smoldering resentments in our lives. This is a vital step in moving forward, free from the burden we've carried around for so long.

Second, we must acknowledge our part in the resentment. This sounds offensive at first, but unless the situation is extreme we have a role in most of our resentments. Sometimes our role may be simply holding onto it for years instead of letting God help us walk freely. We pronounced the verdict and are unwilling to review the judgment.

A simple illustration may help you see how this one-sided condemnation occurs. Suppose that to have a real resentment, the involvement of both the parties must add up to 10. Let's say Bob has offended me, and the offense is clear. On reflection, I have to admit that I had a role in the problem. So Bob's part in the offense amounts to a 7. My part amounts to a 3. Now let's watch what happens.

I wake up the next day, and I get my resentment-thinking going. As I self-righteously review the events, I decide that Bob's role was more like an 8. Mine was only a 2. In succeeding days I keep stewing on it and talking to anyone who agrees with me that Bob is a jerk. Pretty soon his part is a 9. Mine is 1. Before too long, a practicing "resenter" like me, can get to the point where I say "I was standing there minding my own business, and Bob came along and did this terrible thing to me!" I've absolved myself and completely condemned Bob.

Don't think this happens? Be honest. The word resentment comes from two words, re which means again, and sentir which means to feel. A resentment is an offense you feel again and again, and each time you feel it, the truth can get a little bit more distorted.

The way to be free of the resentment is to honestly accept our part, even though it may have been minor. Legalism and unbending judgment distances us from the God of grace, and that's why if we constantly condemn people we're only going to put ourselves in prison. To get past the resentment we need grace. Seeing our part is vital.

The final step must be handled carefully. In prayer ask for God's direction and help. Forgiving the offender is necessary. The New

Testament teaching on this is abundant, and there is no shortcut. We need to forgive. This may mean acknowledging to the offender our part and apologizing without any expectation of their response. We are the ones trying to relieve the burden we have been carrying. We can't expect them to respond by forgiving us, though that often happens.

We'll also find that praying for the offender helps us find relief. Try it! Pray for God to bless them. At first you may not mean it. Pray anyway. Soon the resentment will cool, and forgiveness will follow. And on a purely practical level, if you really want to mess with your enemies, forgive them.

Putting away anything is a process, and that is especially true of resentments. It won't happen overnight, but it needs to happen. We'll walk lighter.

Choosing to Be Grateful

"Be thankful in all circumstances, for this is the will of God in Christ Jesus for you." 1 Thessalonians 5:18

I started my own holiday season a few years ago. It comes around the same time every year. As the earth leans back into autumn and the air breathes a bit cooler we approach one of the most wonderful times of the year: Thanksgiving Advent.

I have come to believe that one day of Thanksgiving is simply not enough. As we have four Sundays to spiritually prepare to celebrate the birth of Christ, I think we need several weeks to reflect on all the ways God blesses us.

The first step in this important spiritual discipline is a simple commitment: *choose to be thankful.* Some choices are presented to us as so easy that we ought to just fall into them. I read recently that thinking positive thoughts is just as easy as thinking negative thoughts. I wish that were true, but it's plainly not. Learning to think differently is simply not a matter of flipping a switch.

However, choosing to be thankful is just about as simple a choice as you can make. It's a combination of awareness and commitment. God *never* leaves us without a reason to be grateful. Never. Even in terribly challenging situations we're not bereft of blessings. We just have to look a little harder, and that takes commitment.

My mother first started showing signs of dementia when I was in Murray, Kentucky. Her condition rapidly declined until I had to move her from her beloved Lexington to an assisted living facility in Murray.

Because of the rushed nature of the move, I wasn't able to obtain a room for Dad in any nursing home in Murray. He had battled MS for nearly 40 years by that time and had reached the point where he needed special care. He would have to stay behind in Lexington for

1-3 months waiting for a place. Leaving him there and taking his wife away was difficult. It's the only time I saw Dad cry, and he even apologized for weeping, fearing that it made things more difficult for me! It was a hard day.

Several weeks after the move I received a call from a nursing home. They had a space, but it was only a temporary room, small and unadorned. But it was available. I went to see the room, and my heart sank. It was concrete block, institutional monochrome, windowless, dimensions maybe 9'x10'. I agreed to take it because I knew Dad would prefer most anything to being separated from Mom.

He was excited when I spoke to him on the phone. I told him of the Spartan arrangements and that it would be temporary until a regular room for him opened up. They couldn't promise how long it would take. Nothing muted his enthusiasm.

I made the four-hour drive to Lexington, bringing with me the youth director at our church in case I needed any help along the way. We loaded all of Dad's belongings into the trunk along with his wheelchair and returned to Murray.

Dad could hardly contain his excitement. You'd think I was taking him on a cruise. By contrast, I was apprehensive, and even more so when we arrived at the nursing home. What if he didn't like it? He would never let on, of course, but I hated the thought of his being disappointed. Life had been particularly hard for him the previous five or so years. He had endured numerous falls, the MS was worse, and the wheel chair had become a permanent part of his life. Surgery to remove a brain tumor had left him weaker. He also endured prostate cancer and glaucoma. I wanted him to at least have a nice place to live, but this wasn't it.

Wheeling him down the hallway of the nursing home I anxiously explained again that the room was very sparse but that eventually there would be a larger one available. I brought him to the doorway. Standing behind him, I looked into the meager room with an unmade, metal-frame bed with support bar running over it. Being too caught up in getting Dad there, I hadn't thought to at least hang some pictures or bring in something to warm up the room. I started again to explain the temporary, stark arrangements, "Dad, it's a small room . . ." Dad knew what I was doing, and he raised his hand for me to stop and said, "But it's nice. I'm sure glad to be here."

Whenever I read a passage of scripture like "Be thankful in all circumstances" (1 Thess. 5:18), I recall Dad's reaction to that little room. Paul's words in that verse usually raise objections. "How can anyone be thankful in all circumstances?" I was blessed to have a father who modeled for me the faith that enables that kind of gratitude.

Life can difficult in a thousand different ways and can turn our focus from the evidences of God's love and grace to every minor irritant, for our normal default setting is complaint. The good news is that we have a choice today and every day. Dad chose to be grateful. He provided a wonderful example. And for that I am grateful.

Joy: The Laughter of the Soul

"These things I have spoken to you that My joy may be in you, and that your joy may be complete." John 15:11

> Joyful, joyful, we adore Thee,
> God of glory, Lord of love;
> Hearts unfold like flow'rs before Thee,
> Op'ning to the sun above.
> Melt the clouds of sin and sadness;
> Drive the dark of doubt away;
> Giver of immortal gladness,
> Fill us with the light of day!

Doesn't that sound absolutely wonderful? Even in reading the words you probably can "hear" that melody. Henry Van Dyke wrote the lyrics in 1907 especially for the final movement of Beethoven's Ninth Symphony. Words and music are glorious and uplifting. The tune matches the text.

We don't hear a great deal about joy today in our apocalyptic culture where fear, anger, and resentment reign. Perhaps we never have, or it's been a very long time. The good news is it's never too late to recover joy.

Joy, after all, is Jesus' goal for us. He said He came that His joy might be in us and our joy might be complete. The Greek word also means perfected. God's goal through His Son is for our perfect joy.

Joy is also second in Paul's list of the fruit of the Spirit, right after love. It's a part of our birthright, not something we seek, but something we apparently are given. For this reason, Paul also exhorted us to be joyful always and in all situations. He seemed quite sure that this constant experience of joy was not merely a goal, but a gift.

In fact, when look closely at the Greek word for grace we find that the idea of gift is inherent in it. Greek is a highly inflected language, meaning that you take a root word, add various prefixes and suffixes and come up with a whole host of related words and nuances.

The root word for joy is from the Greek χαρ (char- in English). We derive some very beautiful and important words from this root: grace, gratitude, gift, forgiveness, and joy are all derived from the same root. Joy, fundamentally, is a product of grace. God gives grace. When we open up to it (hearts unfold!), our natural response is joy. We are tuned to God's grace, and when our minds resonate with grace, joy is inevitable. We feel powerfully connected, accepted, and approved by God. Joy is the laughter of the soul, security in the Father's love, delight in the fellowship of Christ, and the sweet energy of the Spirit.

How many souls laugh today? It seems we've forgotten joy. I simply don't hear too much about joy.

I hear a lot about happiness. I think that's because happiness is much more measureable. If my health is good, my bills paid, my family reasonably happy, if my UK Wildcats win 6 games and go to the Poulan Weedeater Bowl, then I'm happy. Happiness is a checklist, and that's not a bad thing at all, nor is it superficial and unimportant. Happiness has to do with the avoidance of pain and the creation of pleasant circumstances.

But this definition does point to an important difference between happiness and joy. The former is temporal. The latter, eternal. It's so obviously possible to have all the necessities for happiness but no joy whatsoever. That may be the quintessential American experience. We have it all and nothing at the same time.

Joy is so notoriously hard to pin down that it appears to be simply ignored or forgotten even by some of the most careful thinkers of human nature. I read recently that in the 24 volumes of Freud's works there is not a single mention of the word joy, which is ironic since his name means joy. I wonder if that set a standard unwittingly followed by others today.

Whatever the reason, joy does not appear to be a common experience. I believe this is due to a grinding sense of inadequacy people have in their personal theology. Too many people simply do not feel accepted by God. They're keeping score and that always results in a loss. A sense of aloneness follows. Joy seems impossible.

The recovery of joy, or its initial experience, simply relies on the frank acceptance of the fact that God has accepted you. That is the first axiom of grace. Any voice that tells you God is either displeased with you or rejecting you is simply not from God. God is love, pure and simple. And grace is love in action.

Joy, then, is the intersection of God's nature and our openness. We receive gifts. We don't earn them. Freed of the soul-burden of trying to earn God's favor, we can relax in the rhythms of His grace and truly take it easy. Not that we're relieved of the activities of a higher life, but instead of obligations they simply become expressions of who we are and of our resonance with God. We act because we are loved, not the other way around.

Good religion is never about trying to change God's opinion of you. His opinion is settled. The challenge always is to change your opinion of God. Accepting grace fully quiets fears, doubts, anger, frustration, and a whole host of caustic emotions. And it awakens something truly miraculous.

Wherever you are in life, whatever your past may be, the God who created you loves you and delights in you. When you accept that, and often that will need to happen many times a day, your soul will soar and sing and begin to laugh.

So?

"Bless those who persecute you; bless and do not curse them."
Romans 13:14

I listened as a lady described how she was being criticized by someone close to her. The accusations and complaints were untrue, distorted, or one-sided. She complained to a friend about the unfair treatment. After going through the details and defending herself at some length she waited for the friend's affirmation and consolation. Instead, her friend simply said, "So?"

So? sounds flippant, dismissive, uncaring, bordering on cruel. Actually, it's wise. The friend was trying to remind her that the accusations did not ultimately matter. What mattered was her response to them. So? empowers and focuses us on what we can control (only ourselves). Instead of feeling attacked and the need to defend, we neutralize and rise above the criticism.

This skill is enormously difficult, but it's surely part of Paul's meaning in this text. Jesus said the same thing, adding that you are blessed when people persecute and say all manner of lies about you. I suppose most of us secretly wish Paul hadn't written this and Jesus hadn't taught it. It's far more natural to respond in kind, and it feels better for a short time. God, however, has our long-term and best interest in mind.

Think right now of your most virulent critic. You can recall instantly the unfairness you have suffered at his or her hands. You recall the accusations, and you can resurrect the defenses immediately. In fact, just being reminded of your critic may aggravate you for few minutes, hours, or even days. Having that criticism in mind, try a one-word response: So? That little word works in at least three ways to help you.

So? simply means you're a human being, and so far in recorded history every human being has had unfair critics. You are not unique or exempt from the unfairness of other people. However, most of us feel that if other people knew how good we really are then surely they wouldn't be mean to us! Or if everyone understood why we, on exceedingly rare occasions, may act a bit peevish then they would overlook our minor faults and like us.

Let me repeat, you are NOT unique or exempt. We all have unfair critics. We're contractually obligated to have unfair critics, and they're fulfilling their job description when they criticize unfairly. Welcome to the human race. And by the way, it probably will help to remember that we can be just as unfair. We're all broken. Unfair critics are a part of every life.

So? also means you are going to focus on spiritual resources. I'm amazed by how easily a critic can ruin my prayer life. I go to God and complain, which is fine if I leave it there. But usually I end up rehearsing WHAT I SHOULD HAVE SAID. Or I have a running conversation in my mind about what stinging riposte I'll have ready for the next encounter. My prayer time becomes a waste of time.

Critics are good at pushing my buttons, so I have to work on rewiring my buttons. An unfair critic should remind me to pray, not silence my prayers. An unfair critic should remind me of why I read scripture or devotional works. In a world of unfair, unkind, and unrighteous words and actions, I need the Spirit to lift me above the fray. Instead of throwing me off my spiritual disciplines, the unfair critic reminds me of why I need the spiritual disciplines. Don't let the bad words keep you from doing the good things. Keep praying.

Finally, So? means that you can stop living through the opinions of others. Most of us greet one another by saying "How are you?" But judging by the way we live, most of us could more accurately say, "How am I?" We are tied in unhealthy ways to the opinions of other people, and most ironically we are tied to the critics. A hundred people could write that this is a great devotional, one person could write that it stinks. Guess who I'm going to be thinking about at 1:00 a.m.?

But if I trust God to take care of the problems **in me** then I don't have to think about that critic at 1:00 a.m. I can sleep and hope the critic is tossing and turning wondering why I'm not more susceptible to his slings and arrows. More importantly, I can sleep better because I'm no longer consumed with changing my critic.

You have a critic at home? At work? In the rear-view mirror? So? Don't let them affect you. A critic cannot stop us from doing what we need to do. Ultimately, we must listen to God for our value. He is a God of grace, and He approves of you! Life is so much easier when we stop giving power to our persecutors.

I'm Not Ok, and That's a Good Place to Start
(A Lenten GraceWaves)

"Then I acknowledged my sin to You and I did not hide my iniquity; I said, 'I will confess my transgressions to the Lord,' and You forgave the guilt of my sin." Psalm 32:5

<u>I'm OK, You're OK</u> is the title of a self-help book written by Thomas Harris and published in 1967. Harris proposed four life positions revolving around the idea of whether we consider ourselves and others ok. I never read the book, but I want to propose a Lenten version. Because Lent begins with the proposition that we're not ok, let's begin each statement with that confession: I'm not ok.

<u>I'm not ok, but it's not the end of the world.</u>

Admitting I have a problem is really the start of hearing the gospel. I can't really hear the good news until I admit the bad news. The fact is, I'm really not ok. Sin has twisted and distorted me. I'm not what God wants me to be. The cross was necessary, in part, because of what's wrong with Terry Ellis.

I think all of us know deep down that something is terribly wrong. I also think it's a terrible mistake to make our awareness of our brokenness the focus of our religious practices. We don't have to keep confessing sins we've already brought to God. The point here, of course, is that we do need to bring them to God as we would bring a disease to a doctor. We have the diagnosis pretty clearly. Telling God about it doesn't mean we're going to be thrown into hell's pit. It's the beginning of the healing.

God wants me to confess my sins, not to make me feel bad about myself, but because at a very deep level I already feel bad about myself. I know something is wrong, and no amount of "I don't need to feel guilty" is going to solve the problem. I do need to feel guilty when I'm guilty. God won't solve anything in me until I let Him in, and that happens with a simple admission: "I'm not ok." Having made this simple confession of my brokenness I discover that I have not dissolved into a puddle of guilt and self-pity, and neither will you.

Next I turn to…

<u>I'm not ok, and frankly neither are you, but that's none of my business</u>.

My first temptation when I confess my sinfulness is to shift the focus anywhere else. I don't like to think about my brokenness, and I may still not be really convinced that I'm all that badly broken. In fact, you're broken worse than I am! If I can focus on your sinfulness (which is always more obvious to me than mine) then I don't have to worry about mine.

The fact is, of course, you are a mess too, but that's none of my business. I can't make you repent, and I can't change you, so I just need to leave you out of the equation. Lent is very selfish. I have to focus on me, not you. The Bible consistently forbids me from judging for this very reason. I need to stick with the fact that I have a problem, and your problem is none of my concern.

Which leads me to…

<u>I'm not ok, and your opinion of me is none of my business</u>.

One reason I'm so reluctant to admit I have a problem is that I'm afraid you will think less of me if I do. My tendency, therefore, is to cover-up and lift up. I cover up my faults and lift up my virtues. Instead of deflecting, which is what I do when I try to focus on your problem, I am projecting a better person than I am. It's a façade and a lie, and frankly it's exhausting.

But if I divorce myself from your opinion of me, then I'm free. Some people will not like me, and truthfully, I have done some unlikeable things. Those people have a right not to like me, but I have a right not to be tied to their opinion of me. I simply cannot be consumed by what other people think, whether they are right or wrong. My task is to become a better person, and only God can do that. I listen for His voice above all critics, set things right when I'm able, and move on. God's opinion of me matters most.

Which is very good news because…

<u>I'm not ok, but I will be some day.</u>

Again, accepting the fact that I'm broken allows me to focus on God's grace. He has taken care of all the bad in me. My number one task is to confess and live in the grace God offers, for then something truly wondrous happens. God knows I'm not ok, but He's not willing to leave me there. As long as I'm open to His leading and His grace then my residual brokenness is in His hands, and the healing goes on and on.

Grace has a rhythm. God brings me to completion in His way and in His timing. As long as I regularly confess and ask for forgiveness, and mean it, then I'm free to walk with God. Where I am in life right now, and my spiritual state at this moment, is acceptable to God. He's not surprised by where I am, and He's not disappointed. I'm already His, and He is not finished with me. He has already forgiven the guilt of my sin and is in the process of making me new. I'm a work in progress. So I'm not yet all ok, but I will be some day.

God balances a tremendous interest in our present with a solid hope for our future. Thankfully, He's in the business of making all things ok.

The Glimmer of Hope
(An Advent GraceWaves)

"Are you He who is to come or should we look for another?"
Matthew 11:3

God's prophets had a terrible arrest record. Many of them spent time in jail. Others were beaten, and some were killed. Most were unpopular with the people in general as well as the government. Being a prophet was a hard calling and a rough way to get a blessing. John the Baptist learned this first-hand. He was in jail when he sent the question to Jesus, "Are you He who is to come or should we look for another?"

Remember, John was Jesus' cousin. He had proclaimed, "Behold the Lamb who takes away the sin of the world," had baptized Jesus, saw the Spirit descend upon Him as a dove, and heard the words "you are my beloved Son" from heaven. If any man was in a position to embrace complete certainty it was John the Baptist.

At first he probably thought the arrest was a temporary detour. After all, the Messiah was here! He would scatter the brood of vipers and hack down all the trees that bore no fruit. But the snakes were still crawling, the trees were still growing, and John began to doubt.

A little time (and he may have been in prison for two years) in the darkness will do that to even the strongest person, and no one was greater than John. Doubt turned into disappointment, disappointment into discouragement, and discouragement into despair. John began to wonder if his most cherished belief was misguided. He had to ask, "Are you the One?"

Doubt, disappointment, discouragement, despair. Anyone who was spent time in any kind of darkness understands that sad progression. What once might have been a bright certainty of faith turns into a paltry candle, if that. Yet there are many lessons in the shadows. In fact, the most lasting lessons are taught only in the darkness. There's so much we can we learn when the lights are dim.

First, doubt and its depressing cousins do not indicate the absence of light. They underscore the *necessity* of light. Think carefully about this. When you are at your lowest point, you will be tempted to fling away from faith, being convinced that all around you is darkness and darkness is all there is. The light you once saw, you think, was probably not light at all. It was just a delusion, a product of wishful thinking.

I truly believe John was at this point. He might have wondered if anything he had believed in, hoped for, and proclaimed was true. He was not immune to these spiritual struggles. No one is. The greatest saints walked a sorrow-filled path. That's how they became great saints.

When you find yourself in similar shadows you have a crucial decision to make. You must decide if the core convictions you have learned about God are true. Feelings will not change. Evidence still seems very thin. But you have to decide if you're going to keep believing. When faith flickers, you have to cling to a glimmer of hope.

Faith is often simply a decision. It doesn't make sense. People will mock it. You will sometimes wonder if they're right. You just have to decide to believe and keep hoping.

Even at his nadir, John did not give up hope. Not completely. He wondered if his earlier convictions about Jesus were correct, but he also was willing to "look for another." He knew the light had to be there even though he had trouble seeing it. Bad times don't change the fundamental facts about God. The truth of Christ abides, and the present distress does not disprove it. Instead it underscores our need for Him. Do not give up hope even during the most threatening darkness.

Second, even a small amount of light is sufficient to sustain hope, and God never leaves us without that. Hope is the theme of the first week of Advent, and we usually sing sing "O Come, O Come Immanuel." It's in a minor key. We read of the prophets who promised God's intervention but did not know that promise would be kept *centuries* in the future. John's words capture our challenge perfectly. The light during that lone-candle-week of Advent is rather dim. *But it is still light.*

A candle in the depths of Mammoth Cave might appear to be overwhelmed by the cavernous darkness, but it would be sufficient for you to make your way through. If you are surrounded by darkness right now, cling to the glimmer of hope, and look for the light God sends. It may be faint. In fact, it usually is. God loves subtlety and often shows up as a faint shimmer.

The light God sends may come in the form of a hymn in a worship service. A phone call from a friend or family member. It could be a smile, a star, a child, a dog, a moment of stillness. The stillness is most important, in fact. If you sit still in the dark, your eyes grow accustomed to it, and you begin to see things you overlooked before. Whatever form the glimmer takes, do not mourn its meagerness, celebrate its presence! God sent it to help you through today. Just look around, and you will see it.

We see through a glass darkly right now, but it is a glass, and we do see movement on the other side. Seldom is faith either crystal clear or a bonfire, and it's perfectly fine to face that uncomfortable truth squarely. God reveals Himself and His plans incrementally. He gives just enough light to take the next step. Hope keeps you moving.

The glimmer of hope is a promise of a future dawn in a city where there is no sun or moon to shine upon it, for the glory of God will be its light. Until that day we look for the glimmer. It's always there.

If We Knew Their Story...

"Do you see this woman?" Luke 7:44

"Up Close and Personal" was originated by ABC sports icon Roone Arledge in the 1960's as way of making sporting events more intimate for the viewer. One of the keys was providing the background of not only the event, but also the participants.

I grew up watching "Wide World of Sports" and the Olympics when ABC broadcast them. They could run an "Up Close and Personal" segment on some obscure Eastern Bloc athlete and soon I was pulling for the Bulgarian shot putter who was raised on a dairy farm with 11 siblings and a pet Alpaca. Roone was right. If you know the person's story, you end up understanding, and perhaps liking, the person.

This insight explains how God can love each one of us. The backstory of the parable of the two debtors is a perfect illustration. Jesus was at the home of Simon the Pharisee when "a woman of the city, who was a sinner" entered the home and began to weep and anoint Jesus' feet. Simon was stunned and thought to himself that Jesus could not really be a prophet, for if He was then He would know what sort of woman she was and certainly would not allow her to touch Him.

Jesus knew what was going on and told a parable of two debtors, one owing a great deal and the other a relative pittance. Neither could repay, and both were forgiven. It's a great parable of grace, and I've written and spoken on it's meaning many times. If you're spiritually broke then it doesn't matter how much you owe. You've got to rely on grace. Thus, we are all equal in both need and solution.

I want to focus this week, however, on the line Jesus spoke right after the parable: "Simon, do you see this woman?" Of course he did. She was right there in his dining area. He noticed her the moment she set her dirty little foot inside his home. He saw her as clearly as his graceless eyes could focus. He saw her wretchedness, and it repulsed him.

But Simon didn't really *see* her. Jesus did, and He not only saw the sin, He saw the brokenness that lay behind it. He knew her story, all of it, and because of that He loved her.

Isn't it interesting that the one Person, God, who knows us best loves us the most? Isn't it ironic that we are so often afraid of God? That we want to hide from God?

When considering ourselves we tend to operate on the basis of "if you really knew me you wouldn't like me." So we hide our wounds, never talk about our scars, and generally try to keep everyone at arm's length.

When it comes to considering other people, we tend to be like Simon. We see only the failure or irritation and fit them into a little box of contempt. Thus, the woman was a sinner, or the ex-husband is a jerk, or the former friend is a gossip, or the driver behind me is an idiot, etc. With the verdict pronounced, the sentence can be passed, and we can simply dismiss all the irritating, immoral, wicked, and selfish people around us.

And we end up either mighty lonely or insufferably self-righteous, or both.

The story of Jesus, Simon, and the woman teaches that the line of good and evil runs right through each one of us. I can look at the picture of the criminal on the front page of today's paper and be disgusted, rightly so, by what he did. The facts, just the facts, of the crime are clear.

What I can't know is what that criminal's life has been like. What abuse did he endure as a child? What unfair shame does he carry that no one has taken time to lift away? At one point in his life could a loving man or woman really made a difference in the path he took? I can also look at that picture and forget my own evil.

Every "Simon" reading this so far will likely object that I'm providing excuses. No. I'm providing a likely explanation. Evil doesn't breed in a vacuum. It's socially contagious and fed by the evil within each of us.

I'm not suggesting that a crime should not be punished or that evil shouldn't be condemned. All of our actions have consequences, the good ones too. The way of grace is both puzzling and amazing precisely because it looks beyond the surface.

Jesus did *see* the woman in a way that Simon, in his strict legalistic categories, could not. He knew her story, or at least understood that there was a whole lot more to the story than the plain fact that she was a prostitute. Perhaps she had lost her father early in life or been abused by him. Maybe she was married at one point, then her husband died or betrayed or divorced her. Maybe she had a child and this was her means of providing food for their table.

The fact of the matter is, there's not a single person you wouldn't love if you knew their story, up close and personal. Trauma, big T and little t, twists lives in a lot of different ways. Grace has a way of helping straighten out the twists, healing the wounds, and bringing hope to the hopeless.

That's what Jesus is for, and that's what He wants us to be part of. What a different world we would have if we took time to learn each others' stories and got to know each other up close and personal. Knowing everyone's story is plainly impossible, but the next time I want to react to another person with condemnation, irritation, or just plain meanness I hope I can remember there's more to their story. If we knew the story of the people we hate… God does, and He responds with grace.

John Wayne: Prophet

"Look carefully then how you walk, not as unwise men but as wise." Ephesians 5:15

I have a bit of a problem with "everything happens for a reason." I usually hear this as an explanation of some unfortunate, even criminal, event. It's sounds terribly callous to say, but my reaction sometimes is "some things happen because we're really stupid and make dumb decisions."

Turns out, John Wayne was a prophet as well as an all-American hero. In the same vein, he reportedly said, "Life is hard, but it's harder when you're stupid." As with many aphorisms, I don't know if he actually said this or if it's merely attributed to him, but it certainly suits The Duke. (As a kid, I wanted to be like John Wayne when I grew up, but only made it a little past Don Knotts).

Now I don't recommend going around labeling anyone's behavior as stupid. The word is too crass, but the sentiment certainly is true. Life can beat you up when you're walking the straight and narrow, but you don't need to invite the blows by living unwisely.

That's the constant refrain of the biblical prophets and especially clear in the verse from Paul. He often included a section in his letters that addressed practical, daily living, and that is the case in the last two chapters in Ephesians. Based on the deep and sound theology of the first part of his letter, how then should we live? The key is wisdom, literally a right thinking about life and how we should best live it. What direction for life can I glean from Paul and John Wayne?

First, I need a regular reminder to be wise. I have done things in my life I'm not proud of, things that hurt me and other people.

I can recall certain episodes from my teenage years when Dad would shake his head and say "I thought you had better sense than that."

He could have used the word "stupid" and been right on the money. I was unwise.

I still have that ability and the growing record to prove it. We all do to some degree. But our shared stupidity underscores the remarkable nature of God's grace. The fact that we have failed does not invalidate the wise lifestyle, and our shared hypocrisy does not mean we should not strive for the higher life in Christ. God loves us unconditionally, but in His love for us He will not leave us where He found us. He calls us to a higher life. I need to listen for that call and follow.

Second, we must understand God's intention for our living the wise life. God "tuned" us to operate best when we love Him, others, and ourselves. The Christian moral life described in the Bible is always in our spiritual and physical best interest. We have greater peace, bless others, and are generally physically healthier if we walk in the light.

The alignment of joy and the moral life is the overlooked key to the Christian life. Too often, people view God as prudish, a spoil-sport trying to keep us from having any "fun." The exact opposite is true. God is joy. He is peace. And He is holy. He tries to steer us away from behavior that is harmful, to ourselves and others, as He tries to steer us to Him.

It's a dangerous path to treat the moral life as unsophisticated and obsolete. The Creator understands His creations. To really enjoy life, we need to live wisely.

Third, we must never make the moral life the primary focus of faith. Read carefully here, please, otherwise I risk being labeled a libertine. The moral life has some definite parameters, some do's and don'ts, but if that is the primary aim then we risk descending into legalism and becoming either terribly judgmental or chronically unhappy. We can become "good" in the very worst sense of the word.

Paul is our best illustration. In Philippians he wrote that he was blameless under the law. I don't think this was an idle boast. Paul knew how to obey rules. He was scrupulous, i.e. full of scruples, but he lacked love and probably any sense of an abiding spiritual élan.

His life in Christ changed him. God brought him deeply into the heart of grace so that Paul still conformed to a higher standard, but for an entirely different reason. It was an expression of gratitude and love. It was a longing to be like God who resided within Him, not a desperate attempt to impress God or other people.

Fortunately, wisdom is not a function of either intelligence or religiosity. It begins with a simple desire for God, not for what He can do for me, but a sustained longing to know what God is like and what He wants for me. I truly believe that if we pursue faith in this manner then "all these things will be added."

So, pilgrim, everything does happen for a reason. It's incumbent upon me, and every one of us, to make sure those reasons are wise.

Soul Graffiti

"Let us make man in Our image." Genesis 1:26

The three most important questions in life are "Who am I?" "Why am I here?" and "Where am I going?" Notice which one is first. Do you know who you are? The question of identity is the most important. We have to know who we are before we can know our purpose or destiny.

To answer this most fundamental question we simply need to go to the beginning. The very first chapter of the Bible contains a statement of immense power and potential. God made a decision to make us in His image.

Think of that for a moment. There is something very god-like about every human being. While we can't be certain what this "something" is exactly, it definitely separates us from all of creation, and that is the point we must cling to. Something is eternally, immutably, wonderfully divine about every one of us.

All kinds of images come to mind to describe this! God put a little bit of Himself in you. Your spiritual DNA is directly from the Father of Lights. He installed the software at the very beginning. Maybe it's better to say that God installed the operating system. Let's keep working with the metaphors. He put a little heaven in you. I like the way the writer of Ecclesiastes phrased it, "He has put eternity into man's mind" (3:11).

Theologians have puzzled for centuries over what this image is. Again, we simply can't be precise, but I'm certain that it can only be understood in relational terms (as everything about God must be understood). Everything about God's nature and actions have the goal of helping us draw near to Him. So my divine image enables me to know and relate to God.

The image enables us to hear the song of creation itself, every day. We hear not just an echo of God's original creation but we are tuned to the ongoing rhythms of His grace so that we "vibrate" when completely in tune with Him. Most of us experience this as a soul-deep longing for and satisfaction with God alone. "As the deer longs for flowing streams so my soul longs for thee, O God" (Ps. 42:1).

We may try to escape this heavenly music by turning up a lot of the noise of life. I have many times spoken to people who have run from God, flatly denying or dismissing His existence and embracing many forms of chaos. What's supremely interesting to me, however, is that in quiet and reflective moments they all wonder about God. They seem to love "the idea" of God. That primal curiosity is the image singing to them.

Now those who no longer struggle with "the idea" of God often face a problem of spiritual amnesia. We forget what we should remember, and remember what we should forget. We sometimes live as if we have forgotten God. Let's change the metaphor from music to art. The image becomes so marred by the graffiti of fear, anxiety, avarice, resentment, etc. that we forget where we came from. So we forget who we are.

The Bible essentially is a record of God's driving home our identity and trying to restore it. Restoration ultimately is the work of Christ. He erased the graffiti. We must simply accept this grace, embrace who we are in Christ, and follow the Artist.

I've often thought that my task in life is the be a re-minder, that is, one who reminds. So let me remind you today of what the scripture says about you and your image. Each phrase is rooted in scripture or a scriptural idea.

You are a child of God, one of His sons or daughters. He is your Daddy, your Papa, the One who never mistreated, neglected, or abandoned you.

You are redeemed, that is, set free of all the bondage of your past. You don't need to spend time in regret about the past or attempt to hide it. Redemption is true and complete freedom.

You are holy, blameless, and righteous before God *through* Christ. The fact that you do not feel holy, or even act holy at every turn, doesn't change the fact that God sees perfectly what you will be in the end.

You are chosen. God picked you. He adopted you and wants you in His family.

You are a new creation. Every day you have an opportunity to start your life over. Every day. Even when you have fallen every day previously.

You are completely forgiven. A young woman recently asked me if I thought God forgave her for her abortions. God forgives all, I assured her. I wonder if that was what kept her from seeing and rejoicing in God's image in her? I hope she does now.

Trust me that I could go on and on. The Bible is quite clear about who you are. A good summary might be Isaiah 43:4 where God said, "You are precious in My eyes, and honored, and I love you."

God calls constantly to the image in you. He sings to you. Woos you. Speaks softly to you. He erases all the ugly smudges, repairs all the painful gouges, and brings back the wondrous color of His image in you.

The Most Important Breakfast Ever

"When they got out on land, they saw a charcoal fire there, with fish lying on it, and bread." John 21:9

Breakfast, they say, is the most important meal of the day. I tend to eat breakfast like my dog eats breakfast: I have the same thing every morning. So while breakfast may be an important meal, it is hardly life changing, and mostly it's forgettable.

John 21:9 is a breakfast text. It describes a setting for breakfast. At first it doesn't appear to be highly significant or meaningful. I doubt anyone ever memorized it for a Bible drill. It's not included in any great devotional that I know of. But if you learn the lesson taught at this simple gathering, then you may see that this is the most important breakfast in history. In fact, I doubt you'll ever forget it or will ever look at a backyard cookout the same way.

The scene is the shore of the Sea of Galilee at some undetermined time after Jesus' resurrection. "They" are the disciples, and the fire was prepared by Jesus. The narrative order in John's gospel is very important. In chapter 20, Jesus had appeared a few times, breathed the Holy Spirit on the disciples, and commissioned them to go out and change the world. After an appearance to Thomas, the 20th chapter ended on a very high note, full of promise.

Or so it seems. Though John 20:31 does sound like a fine ending, we find chapter 21. Peter, the disciples' de facto leader, said, "I am going fishing," and a handful of the disciples joined him and returned to their previous work. They fished all night and caught nothing. Then in the early morning mists they saw a figure on the shoreline they soon realized was Jesus. Peter, always impulsive, jumped in and swam to the shore. And that brings us back to the fire and the fish.

You see, Jesus had prepared this fire so He could cook a breakfast for these hungry disciples. But it was not just any fire. The text is quite specific. John used a word that we find only twice in the New Testament, *anthrakia*, a charcoal fire. He wanted us to know Jesus had prepared a charcoal fire.

That's interesting. Along the shores of a lake (the Sea of Galilee is a large fresh water lake) you can always find plenty of driftwood. It has dried out in the sun and is perfect for a fire. But Jesus did not use driftwood for this fire. He used charcoal. Now we have to use our imagination here, but it might be fun, so play along. Before Jesus left heaven again to make this appearance, He got some charcoal. Maybe He had Gabriel go for it. "I need some charcoal," He might have said, and Gabriel obeyed. He was a bit puzzled, but he obeyed. And so Jesus appeared on the shore and built a charcoal fire.

Now let's get back to the narrative. Recall that Peter had jumped out of the boat and swam ashore. He crawled up on the beach and ran to Jesus. He saw the fire, and, more importantly, I'm sure he *smelled* the fire. Charcoal has a distinct smell, doesn't it? Not like wood at all. Peter smelled the charcoal fire. One of the most powerful memory triggers is the sense of smell. A certain aroma will fire synapses and take you back to an event associated with that smell.

My mother wore White Shoulders perfume. I got her a bottle every Mother's Day. When she died I found unused bottles of White Shoulders. She always graciously accepted my gift as if it was precisely what she needed. My point, however, is that if I smell White Shoulders perfume today the memory-construct in my mind takes me right back to Dottie Ellis.

Remember I said that the word *anthrakia* is only used twice in the New Testament? The first time is in John 18:19 where Peter stood and warmed himself while denying that he even knew Jesus. That was a charcoal fire.

Don't you think that when Peter smelled that breakfast fire on the shores of the sea, he might well have remembered the last charcoal fire he stood by? Don't you think that he remembered at that moment the denials and felt the shame? Don't you think that is probably why he went fishing in the first place?

Shame, even the kind we earn, is a heavy burden. We're simply not meant to carry it around with us for a lifetime. Too often we do. I think Peter crawled onto that shore with a load of shame in tow.

John 21 is best remembered for Jesus' asking Peter three times if he loved Him, Peter affirming three times that he did, and Jesus telling him three times to go and get back to work feeding and tending the sheep. A threefold grace for a threefold denial, prefaced by a charcoal fire that would drive home the genuineness of that grace. The literary symmetry is a beautiful and unmistakable reflection of Jesus' intent.

Peter went fishing because he believed that was the only thing he could do well. Jesus knew better. He knew Peter loved Him. He knew Peter's faults, and He knew Peter's gifts. He knew what Peter could become through grace. And Jesus knows all of these things about you as well.

Sometimes we shy away from God because of shame. We're convinced God is disappointed in us, and so we have pulled in on ourselves. You may feel that way this right now. If so, come to the charcoal fire. Remember that God is not surprised by a single stumble on your part. In fact, He meets each failure with a grace that is so puzzling, so limitless, so real that all of us limping saints can find courage in that grace to get up and get back to life. Peter did, and so can you.

www.ingramcontent.com/pod-product-compliance
Lightning Source LLC
Chambersburg PA
CBHW052159110526
44591CB00012B/2009